SHADOW OF MY SHADOW

MY SHADOW

SHADOW OF

SHADOW OF
MY SHADOW

JENNIFER DOYLE

Duke University Press Durham and London 2024

© 2024 Duke University Press. All rights reserved
Printed in the United States of America on acid-free paper ∞
Project Editor: Bird Williams | Designed by Aimee C. Harrison
Typeset in Untitled Serif by Copperline Book Services

Library of Congress Cataloging-in-Publication Data
Names: Doyle, Jennifer, author.
Title: Shadow of my shadow / Jennifer Doyle.
Description: Durham : Duke University Press, 2024. |
Includes bibliographical references and index.
Identifiers: LCCN 2023042685 (print)
LCCN 2023042686 (ebook)
ISBN 9781478030669 (paperback)
ISBN 9781478026426 (hardcover)
ISBN 9781478059707 (ebook)
Subjects: LCSH: Doyle, Jennifer. | Nassar, Larry—Trials,
litigation, etc. | Ferrante, Elena. Amica geniale—Criticism,
Textual. | Sexual harassment. | Stalking victims. | Sexual
harassment in education—United States. | Sexual harassment
in sports—United States. | BISAC: SOCIAL SCIENCE /
Feminism & Feminist Theory | EDUCATION / Schools /
Levels / Higher
Classification: LCC HD6060.3 . D68 2024 (print) |
LCC HD6060.3 (ebook) | DDC 331.4/133—dc23/eng/20240501
LC record available at https://lccn.loc.gov/2023042685
LC ebook record available at https://lccn.loc.gov/2023042686

Cover art: Aimee Goguen, stills from *cloud and shadow
animation*. Courtesy of the artist.

CONTENTS

ACKNOWLEDGMENTS

A FEW CLOSE FRIENDS MADE significant contributions to this book's development. I would not have been able to take up harassment as a subject in my work were it not for years of conversation with John Andrews, Kathleen McHugh, and Jasbir Puar. Dominic Johnson coached me through my writing about Adrian Howells and heard quite early versions of this work over the years. Sarah Miller lent her significant editorial expertise to the writing of "A Pain in the Neck." I am particularly grateful to Hedi El Kholti, who encouraged me to take up these subjects and published *Campus Sex, Campus Security*, which is, in many ways, this book's companion.

When we go through things, many of our friends go through them too. They see different sides of it—the raw trauma, the logistical nightmare, the surreal hilarity—a few see all of it.

Friends who worked it out with me include Ron Athey, Nao Bustamante, Gavin Butt, Joshua Chambers Letson, Peter Coviello, Robb Hernández, Amelia Jones, Sarah Kessler, Kevin Kopelson, David Kurnick, Ming Yuen S. Ma, Jonathan Maghen, Molly McGarry, Mandy Merck, Giles Miller, Ricardo Montez, Tavia Nyong'o, Michelle Raheja, Emma Stapely, Jim Tobias, and Karen Tongson. Deborah Willis dedicated herself to getting our department through harassment-related crises, including mine. George Haggerty, a friend and mentor who died just as I was finishing this book, attended the interview held around my case at school and also, importantly, invited me to coteach a seminar on Eve Kosofsky Sedgwick's work. I shared the most, however, with José Muñoz: he was my ideal conversation partner and, a decade on, I still miss him.

Many people let me share this work at their institutions and gave me much-needed editorial support. "A Pain in the Neck" was first shared at my second home, Human Resources Los Angeles. This text was originally published as "Letting Go" in *Insecurity*, an anthology developed from a tremendous conference at the Center for 21st Century Studies and the University of Wisconsin, Milwaukee, edited by Richard Grusin. Colleagues (faculty, staff, and students) at the following campuses hosted lectures, workshops, and shared recommendations with me: University of California, Berkeley; University of California, Davis; University of California, Los Angeles; University of Chicago; McGill University; Hobart and William Smith Colleges; Vassar College; New York University; University of Illinois, Urbana-Champaign; the Hammer Museum; Rutgers University; Concordia University; the English Institute; and the University of Essex. Feedback from audiences at SUNY Stony Brook and at the University of Alberta transformed this project. Ann Pellegrini invited me to return to my interest in psychoanalytic theory with an invitation to speak at a conference honoring Muriel Dimen: this led to my work on paranoia. Robyn Wiegman invited me to contribute to a special issue of *differences* dedicated to #metoo and the problem of sexual panic. In that same year, Kyla Wazana Tompkins reached out to ask if I would contribute work to the English Institute's conference on truth-telling. These two invitations led to the writing of two of the chapters in this book ("Harassment and the Privileges of Unknowing" and "Alethurgy's Shadows"). A writers residency at the Banff Center for Creativity led to this book's completion. I am deeply grateful for the weeks I spent there in March 2022. I am deeply grateful to Hal Sedgwick for our conversations about Eve, and to the archivists at the Sallie Bingham Center for Women's History and Culture for their dedication to making her papers available.

Finally, I want to acknowledge a special group of graduate students who helped me reconnect with graduate pedagogy and with my writing: José Alfaro, Sarah Buckner, Mack Gregg, Rudi Kraeher, Hannah Manshel, and Miranda Steege. This book is dedicated, with all my heart, to them.

INTRODUCTION

I f all you knew about stalking was what you learned from *Law & Order*, *Dirty John*, or *Snapped*, you would think that most victims are terrified that they will be killed. There is a strong relationship between stalking and violence. Murder victims are often stalked before the big event. But this is not what keeps a victim up at night. When asked to describe what most haunts them, victims lead not with the fear that they will be hurt. They lead with the anxiety of not knowing what is going to happen; right behind that is the fear that it will never end.[1] These are the conditions of being afraid of life.

Victims describe the experience as having reformatted their sense of self.[2] That was certainly true for me. I was stalked by a student. At work, I was caught in the maw of campus procedure. The unnerving forms of fear, anxiety, and distrust that define the experience of being stalked migrated into my workplace. What happened was painful and bizarre. It disturbed my relationship to writing, teaching, and mentoring. I tried to find ways to restore my relationship to my job and then struggled to accept that in some important ways the damage is permanent.

As you will learn, my writing became the scene of a compound form of violation. When I look back on this time, I think of a rape narrative cliché: the shower scene in which the victim scrubs and scrubs as if she were trying to shed her skin. I used to find these scenes ridiculous—they are so often repeated—but then I caught myself doing my own version of it: scrubbing my writing of the personal voice that otherwise characterized my work. I do this most when I am writing from the place that was violated by what happened. Although personal experience led me to research subjects like harassment and paranoia, when I first wrote about these things I withdrew from the page. I worked at erasing my tracks, adopting a depersonalized voice that was me, and not-me. This is why I've made liberal use of the first person in what you've read so far. I am drawing that person back onto the page.

When I write about this sphere of experience, I confront things that are particular to the situation of the harassed. Creepy energy clings to victims. It is hard to write about harassment without drawing from the economies of sensation that amplify its debilitating effects. I've already done this: these opening paragraphs play to the inherent interest of a stalking narrative. Before we continue, let me dial things back. This person stopped harassing me years ago. Being stalked wasn't the worst thing that's happened in my life. If murder victims are often stalked, stalking victims are rarely murdered. On college campuses, most stalking behavior toward teachers is fleeting, lasting just a few weeks or months. People go through far worse than what I endured. The fact that this person was a student and not a former partner, for example, mitigated the invasiveness of the experience for me. The person who stalked me is not my enemy.

If there is a gothic dimension to the story of what happened to me, it resides not in the figure of a monster but in the paranoid environment of a large, deeply hierarchical institution like a university. This book describes what we lose when harassment ecologies consume us. Each chapter was carved out from the cluster of problems generated by sexualized forms of harassment and bias, and by the situation of writing from my experience and about my own case. In writing this, I have needed to confront my anger and interrogate my aims. For example: when I write as a victim of harassment, I am tempted to present myself as an aggrieved maverick pursuing a tough line of inquiry. I plead my case and ride a wave of self-righteous anger for an hour or two, and then I am beached. While a sense of grievance might be initiated by an actual wrong, it might also be sustained by a sense of entitlement—in that voice, I reconstruct the scene of my betrayal and lament the world that I was promised and denied. My modes of address are off—I am writing not for a reader but for the person who refuses to listen, who abandons my case and turns their back on me. I cannot sustain that voice, so I abandon ship. I come back and sift through the wreckage, plucking out the sentences that argue, plead, and complain. They are sour bubbles of grievance.

Those forms of grievance characterize the most visible writing about sexual harassment and Title IX—stories about feminists accused of harassment, women accused by men, professors lamenting student hysteria, cries of censorship. Popular, widely read articles about specific cases can be characterized by devastating forms of carelessness. This writing thrives on melodramas of uncertainty ("he said/she said") and responds to harassment cases with a scramble for the nearest moral high ground. It is not supported by investigation, research, or even fact-checking.[3] Behind the discourse of harassment—by which I mean the narrative frameworks that shape the experience of and ideas about harassment—are assumptions about the relationship of sex and truth. These assumptions normalize the sense that, when it comes to sex, nothing is knowable, and, at the same time, they laminate the truth of sex to the obscene. Within these structures, sex "appears . . . as an especially dense transfer point for relations of power."[4] It is simultaneously invested with the force of the unspeakable and rendered into a privileged site for heroic truth-telling—this contradiction is weaponized within a harassment ecology. In those instances, victims are positioned as against sex. They are characterized as prudes and hysterics, as overly fragile, or, more brutally, as liars.

The uncertainties and contradictions that haunt the reception of stories of harassment are effects of harassment itself. Harassment's intensities can make it feel like the truth is not only unknowable but irrelevant. This does not mean that the identity of harassment's agents and objects is beyond knowing and saying. But that truth is sometimes disavowed by people who harass and by an abuser's community (this is the subject of chapter 4, which takes up a complaint filed against Larry Nassar that was dismissed by his community). Some people, furthermore, are driven to harass because they feel persecuted and harassed by others. It may be that nothing you say will convince them that the person they are harassing (or the system) isn't out to get them (this dynamic shaped my own case and is the focus of chapter 3, on paranoia).

Harassment is intimate and intensely social. The truth of a harassment case nests in the platform through which that case emerged—for example, the campus, the family, the workplace. Harassment is a nonconsensual form of relation in which a whole scene collaborates. A focus on the monstrosity of the abuser can deflect and contain the ongoing crisis that abuse and the administration of a case present for victims and their workplaces, schools, and homes. The full truth of a harassment case is not guaranteed by the naming of victim and abuser. Harassment is a toxic feature of social ecology: anti-harassment work is fundamental to the cultivation of a good work environment and livable life. Harassment flourishes in neglected spaces, and it is a necessary feature of discriminatory structures. Harassment digs into us at exactly the point at which work and life, public and private converge.

The environment around a harassment case can be so brutalizing that people instinctively back away from everyone associated with it: this fact has been made worse by social media platforms engineered to cultivate outrage, fear, and dread. Stories about campus sexual harassment break on blogs and then appear in *Inside Higher Education* and the *Chronicle of Higher Education*, trade platforms that convert a grievance, a rumor, a complaint into a news story. Then, if the accused is famous enough and the campus elite enough, the fact that these stories were published in those venues is covered by the *New York Times*, and then we get think pieces, threads, more blog posts, and so on. Investigative journalism about sexual harassment cases in higher education has shifted public awareness, but victim-centered, grounded, and complex investigative reporting is, by its very nature, anti-sensationalist.[5] That reporting holds far less grip on our imaginations than writing that allows us to purge our sense of guilt and shame. The news of a harassment case arrives as a scandal, the exposure of which is offered to us as if it were, in and of itself, a solution. The truth of harassment, however, is that it is baked into many of the systems that govern us, and the scandal economy that grows around it is a part of those systems.

Our sexual lives unfold within the social systems into which we are born, and against which many of us struggle. Love, shame, beauty: these things are material expressions of those systems, as is a sense of family, race, and sex. The shape and direction of desire, its objects, the sense of what satisfaction is, whose desires matter, who gets to have or to be family, what pleasures are good and attainable, what pleasures are forbidden and unspeakable — these modes of relation and systems of value are local and have histories. Our lives are material expressions of evolving systems of value that precede us, that conjure and constitute us. This is why harassment matters so much, and why sexualized forms of harassment are so debilitating. It is a vehicle through which people abuse power, steal and hoard resources, and render people unable to act or engage in collaboration and the work of social transformation.[6]

When you file a federal workplace complaint (as I did), you have to give your grievance a material shape that makes sense to the systems governing your labor. This can be an exercise in consciousness-raising regarding the way race and sex cement or slice through your psychic investment in the promises of an institution. The toxic forms of grievance I describe above—forms of grievance that have, at times, grabbed me by the ankles—are underwritten by the promises of institutions. Some of these, like a sense of basic safety, are necessary to our work. Other promises, those of recognition, reward, and something I have described elsewhere as a sense of security, are grand and available only to the most entitled.[7] I have needed to ask myself what it is I actually want and need from the institution for which I work.

The experience of harassment is so much bigger, so much more diffuse than the forms of harm those processes are designed to recognize. *Shadow of My Shadow* accounts for the things I could not articulate within those kinds of structures. In writing this, I have had to ask myself, what did I lose, actually? What is this form of grief, and why is it so hard for me to name it? The opening chapter, about a conversation with the artist Adrian Howells, takes up those questions. That event was the first time I spoke in public about how much being stalked was impacting my work. Written after Howells died in 2014, this chapter is about grief wrapped in grief. "A Pain in the Neck," this book's second chapter, addresses my experience as a stalking and harassment victim. I struggled over this chapter's placement: I have sandwiched this story in between chapters that feel less exposing and less implicated in the toxic ecology of sensation that blooms around stalking victims. Readers who want to read this narrative first are welcome to do so—I want you to feel, however, that this is not where the story starts for me. It starts with the attempt to express how I was changed. "A Case of Paranoia," the third chapter, grew out of a forensic curiosity. I wanted to understand complaint pathology and the paranoid character of nearly all discourse about harassment. I wanted to understand the paranoia that flooded my life.

The last two chapters of this book represent the kind of writing I produced when I wanted to disappear. I published *Campus Sex, Campus Security* in 2015. That book applies what I was learning as a victim to the networked crises gripping college campuses. In a series of brief reflections on cases of police violence, sexual abuse, and privacy violation, I address the amplification of raced and gendered forms of vulnerability, the revictimization of people fighting harassment and abuse, the securitization of the campus, and the ongoing assault on public education in the United States. I lean heavily on the literature for other people's cases—a student at the University of California, Los Angeles; a student at Rutgers University; students at the University of California, Davis, and at Pennsylvania State University; and a faculty member at Arizona State University. In the book's preface, and at the request of my editors, I mentioned the fact that I was stalked and explained that this experience was important to the development of the book. That was all I said about my own case—at the time, harassment was so prevalent in my life that I was afraid that writing in any more detail about my experiences at work would trigger more harassment, not just of me but of students in my department. None of that book's case studies resemble my own, but they allowed me to share some of the wisdom that grew out around the administration of my case and drew me, as a scholar, into new spaces of inquiry. Because it is rooted in a case study, the fourth chapter of this book, "Harassment and the Privileges of Unknowing: The Case of Larry Nassar," is quite similar to *Campus Sex, Campus Security*. I tell the story of a complaint filed against Nassar by Amanda Thomashow and dismissed by administrators at Michigan State University. The scale of Nassar's abuse is hard to comprehend: over decades, while embedded in the world of elite gymnastics and college sports, he abused hundreds of girls and women. This chapter is a study of one document at the center of one case of what trauma studies scholars have termed "institutional betrayal."[8] I write there about a single case that has been subsumed by a story of serial abuse. We have not only the proliferation of victims around Nassar but the proliferation of abusive doctors working for decades within institutions, producing yet more victims. Every sexual harassment complaint, every instance of sexual assault raises this problem of the relationship of individual and systemic violation.

It is hard to center our thinking on victims, especially when confronted with so many. The last chapter of this book is a companion to my writing about the Nassar case: the two essays were written alongside each other. Elena Ferrante's *Neapolitan* Novels center on a friendship between two women that formed when they were little girls. "Alethurgy's Shadows" reads Ferrante's work a little against its grain, using the novels to consider how sexualized forms of violence shape our relationships with each other, especially as we settle into fantasies about each other's truth. We can fail each other when shared senses of vulnerability are contained and managed by projection, disavowal, and denial. The need to be *not her*, meaning, not a victim, hardens into a refusal and sets the limits of who we are to each other and what we do for each other. Those modes of distancing are defense mechanisms. They represent an integration of feelings of loss, betrayal, and anger into a paranoid relationship of the self to others—this distancing gesture structures not only intimate networks of love and family but also relationships to the organizations, groups, and institutions in and for which we work.

I conclude this book by turning to the moment I think of as the beginning of this story. There, I try to stitch my relationship to my work back together, this time with the help of my teacher, Eve Kosofsky Sedgwick, whose work is threaded throughout this book.

1

ON THE DISTANCES
BETWEEN US

One afternoon, in the fall of 2011, the artist Adrian Howells and I had a long, long talk. He was at home in Manchester, and I was in London. As we spoke, I walked the perimeter of a small garden, circling a tree. Adrian had a beautiful, lilting voice and a glittering eloquence that made talking on the phone with him intensely pleasurable.

We were supposed to appear together at a conference to have a conversation about the personal quality of our work. But as the event approached, he let the conference organizers know that he would not be attending.[1] He was just emerging from a deep depression. He could not be on stage, but, he thought, he could talk with me on the phone, and we could broadcast his voice to the audience. Before we did that in public, the two of us needed to connect, to explore what we could say to each other and what we would be willing to share with an audience.

Adrian's work unfolded within the space of the live encounter, often taking forms that seemed to reduce, as much as possible, the distancing effects of theatricality in favor of what he described as an "accelerated intimacy." He held you, washed your feet, shared feelings with you. Adrian took in your presence: the spaces created by his performance practices were intimate.

Adrian's practice was rigorous—in a one-on-one encounter with him, there was no hiding—but it was also profoundly forgiving. My encounters with his performances transformed my scholarship—something about the way he was with me, as an audience member and participant, gave me permission to acknowledge the limits and failures of the way I had been thinking, and to think again from those failures, to work them through. It made me want to translate that into my work—meaning, it made me want to create a similar experience for the reader and for my students.

We were put in conversation with each other because people experience his work as personal. Adrian's performances are often autobiographical; he was also known for staging one-on-one encounters with him that were carefully intimate. At that point, I had not written much that was autobiographical, but the voice I use as a writer can feel quite personal. That effect is enabled by style and gender. I share myself easily, or I used to. I situate myself, as a critic and as a person, in my work. My book *Hold It against Me* grew from writing about my failure to see Adrian's performance *Held*. I introduce the book with a story about the emotional roller coaster of missing my appointment. The idea of that performance genuinely challenged me—acknowledging and confronting my failure in that context is essential to that book's project, which is the creation of a critical language for addressing the relationship between emotion and difficulty in art. As a scholar, I wanted to create a space in which the reader might be invited to reflect on their own limits through an encounter with mine. My work, and Adrian's, can feel personal, and sometimes is personal. But what does this mean? Who is the person we encounter in writing, or in performance? People see our work as about us, but they also find themselves in our work. In the latter situation, is it that they identify with us, as people? Or is it that they find themselves not in the figure of our person, but in its traces, or perhaps in something more abstract—in the texture or affective environment of our work, in the shape of a sentence I wrote, or in the sound of Adrian's voice? Or is it that the subject of our work—loneliness, desire, gender, for example—renders the experience of reading it personal, because the stakes are necessarily personal and, often, quite high?

Adrian and I were both interested in how we address people through our work, and we had both run up against the wild properties of language as a site of intimacy and distance. Words at once carry our selves, and don't. They can open us up to each other, but they can also take on the aspect of walls.

When we talked, we were both in strange places with regard to our work. This made for a good conversation, one which, I think, surprised the audience. Afterward, we were invited to edit and publish the transcript. We avoided returning to it. Our interactions around the possibility of transcribing the conversation were a little cantankerous until we both realized we shared the same hesitancy. At some point we made the decision to let it go.

Adrian died by suicide in March 2014. Not long after his death, I was asked to revisit our dialogue. Reading the transcript of our conversation required a kind of dissociation. That situation mirrors the problems that we explored together—the challenge of being, the difficulty of being present to others, and the limits of words. We'd both resisted returning to the conversation because it was such a hard conversation. I wrote a version of this essay instead—it is an account of being vulnerable, caught out, in your work (the subject of our conversation).[2] It is also an attempt to realize, in writing, the grounding truth of loss.

I want to create a space in which one might think, and think with feeling; to think about, and with, the experiences of being with Adrian Howells because this is central to his practice. Adrian's work confronts the distance between us. It is concerned with the situation of facing and addressing each other. I remember a moment in one performance in which he faced me, wearing headphones. He was listening to music that made him cry; it was music drawn from the archive of a painful love relation. I remember lying in a bed while he read a Walt Whitman poem to me and the warmth I felt in that moment.

The memory of Adrian's work makes me want to write in a way that performatively enacts the intimacy of thinking with someone. In this case, the "thinking with someone" is you and me. I've slipped into Adrian's place—but who am I to do that? And who am I, to you? Or you, to me?

Is this too much? Maybe I have not done enough to make that turn to you feel inviting. Or perhaps I have done too much. The turn to the audience or reader can become a turning away—a sense of *me* can be so strong it precludes the possibility of the reader finding space in the writing for themselves. The "personal" of *I, you*—even *we*—in the wrong environment, in an environment that is, perhaps, too proper, too bounded, may not be enough to unravel the disciplinary protocol, the demand of a report. In which case, these pronouns feel hollow. Or perhaps, now that you know that I am a stalking victim, you can feel the creepy possibility embedded in my turn to *you*—for I have a reader who is sure that my *you* is hers alone. When Adrian and I talked, we connected across our different *you*-and-*me*s.

He and I shared a desire to work in the space of the performative: a space in which modes of expression do more than indicate, relate, or tell. In a traditional, scholarly essay the voice of the author is dissolved into things like literature review (an overview of previous work on the subject) and argument. The writing can be flat as its poetics are subordinated to its communicative function. The poetic gives us a sense of mind—tone, grammar, syntax, pacing, even the mouthfeel of a word—this is, for me, what makes reading feel like thinking. We don't create that sense of thinking just by telling the reader "I think X," just as we don't argue by writing "in this essay I argue X." Jean-Luc Nancy writes that it is not "enough to dress discourse in the form of an address (for me to address you with the familiar 'you' [*tu*] the whole way through)."[3] Nancy is interested in the address that allows us to feel the material situation of addressing and being addressed, what the poet Claudia Rankine (borrowing from Judith Butler) describes as "the condition of being addressable."[4] For me, this is the writing that works on you as you read. You can't make your writing do that for every reader, but you can amplify the conditions that make such a thing possible. You can engineer its possibility. In this form, Nancy writes, "thinking itself addresses itself to 'me' and to 'us' at the same time; that is, thinking addresses itself to the world, to history, to people, to things: to us."[5] This kind of writing gives the reader a sense of the work flowing with them into the world as "an address that comes to us from everywhere simultaneously, multiplied, repeated, insistent, and variable, gesturing only toward 'us' and toward our curious 'being with one another,' [*être-les-uns-avec-les-autres*] toward our understanding one-another."[6]

A treatise, a scholarly essay expressed in a traditional format, for example, is much more solid. It offers you discrete objects of thought. It's easier to say what its argument is. It's easy to say what it's about. And yet this kind of writing is often quite difficult to read. It does not always have (or need) a strong sense of story. The traces of the author, as a particular person, are minimized in order to make room for authority—I do this in the other chapters in this book, in the writing which I've scrubbed clean. Glitches, like a jarring change in tense (a problem here, as I write over the space of Adrian's death) are smoothed over; repaired. Our encounter (as writer and reader) is generalized in the "neutralization of address" and dissolved by a "subjectless discourse," a professional language.[7] The thinking that takes up thinking as an object of thought, the writing that addresses writing, the address that addresses, appears as something else.

When we staged our conversation, I sat on a couch onstage, and we communicated via Skype, using only audio. Adrian's voice was broadcast into the theater. The conference was held in a medium-sized theater, small enough to feel intimate, especially because the audience was drawn from a tight-knit community of performance artists and performance studies scholars. Many of us knew most of the people in the room.

We cycled a few times through stories describing our own struggles with words. He had been thinking about the distancing effects of language and was enjoying the wordless forms of disclosure that could unfold in certain performance actions. He gave the following example:

> I particularly became imbued with that idea when I did research for what ended up becoming *The Pleasure of Being: Washing, Feeding, Holding*. I had a gentleman, who was about 22 stone, sitting on my lap, and I had my arms around him and we sat there for about 20 minutes in silence. I became very aware that he wasn't really giving me all of his weight and that actually he was trying to keep weight on his left foot, off of my body. But I had asked him to absolutely sit on my lap and that was what I was expecting to experience.
>
> But actually in that twenty minutes what was fascinating to me was that there was a dialogue that went on, there was an exchange that went on between our two bodies, no words were exchanged, and I really felt strongly afterwards when he left me that in many ways he said more about how he felt about being who he was, his self image and what have you, through the silence and the bodily interactions that we had than he would ever possibly be prepared to say verbally. And so I thought confession, or the idea of confession, is a very delimiting term, and actually I think what's happening much more is a kind of revelation rather than a confession in that sort of context. And I also think that confession is inextricably linked to religion and ideas of shame and guilt and I wanted to move away from an understanding of confession from that sort of context and background.[8]

Confession structured Adrian's performances as Adrienne (e.g., *An Audience with Adrienne*) and many of his one-on-one encounters (e.g., *Adrienne's Dirty Laundry Experience*, *Fourteen Stations in the Life of Adrian Howells*). It is the explicit form for a whole category of his work. If, in those performances, he wanted to remove self-disclosure from institutional structures (religious, psychiatric) that saturate such scenes with "shame and guilt," he also wanted to interrupt or at least slow down the equation of self-disclosure and confession that structures so much mass and social media and that churns out versions of the authentic self as a rapidly consumed commodity. A pileup of throwaway selves. There is, he said in other interviews and conversations (in which he sounds very much like a twentieth-century person), no real catharsis in those forms.[9]

Within an institutional framework, confession marks out the deficiencies and needs of the self in order that one might be forgiven, or healed. Confession can enable collaboration in the experience of sharing each other's worries, burdens, and limits. In a dialogue with Deirdre Heddon, Adrian explains that as he expanded the situation and meaning of confession in his practice, he realized that he "had used 'talking' as a mask, something to hide behind."[10] In our conversation, Adrian described himself as feeling "sick of [his] own voice."

Before our public conversation, we talked for a long while about our struggles. I confessed my revulsion, after the disastrous end of a romance, at nearly everything I had written to my lover, but especially the sentences I wrote to him when things were falling apart. To this day, it pains me to look at that archive. That writing is so needy—every sentence so crafted, so full of hope that it might draw him to me. (The hubris!) As if that wasn't bad enough, at the time Adrian I spoke, I was just barely recovering from being stalked. That person sent emails that mirrored my writing back to me in what felt like a zombie takeover of my work. My writing self came back to me as a psychotic ghost, filled with needs I did not understand and could never meet.

If there is anything to be said about growing older, depending on how things are going, time's passage can increase the likelihood of knowing/feeling that you will not feel however you feel forever—this was also something Adrian and I talked about as we addressed our struggles with depression (him) and anxiety (me). When it feels like those states will never end, they are unbearable. Until I was stalked, I had a playful relationship to sentimentality in general, and to my own in particular. But I've not had a feeling in the same way since all of those things happened, and I'm not sure I will ever get those feelings back.

Putting ourselves out there does not always have happy results. Perhaps because we have to work so hard to advocate for performance as a creative and scholarly practice, or for sex-centered thought as carrying wisdom and value, we do not speak as often as we should about the frightening side of putting ourselves in our work. The space of emotion that our work describes (or enables, or creates)—the space that unfolds in a reader or audience member as their feeling—holds pockets of alienation and loneliness. We hold some of those spaces inside us, and sometimes we find ourselves caught out—sliced by other people's madness, anger, shame, and disgust. One need not, in fact, make work that is particularly autobiographical in order to encounter the worst in one's readers or audience. The work need only be just queer enough, or just Black or Brown or feminine enough.

The roots of queer theory are anchored in feminist, antiracist, and LGBT resistance to those disciplinary discourses that sift the personal from the professional, which abject all forms of reproductive labor (e.g., nurturing, caring), and pathologize those who organize their lives around something other than monogamy, marriage, reproduction, and home ownership. The earliest articulations of queer theory emphasized the queering of theory and understood this to be something enacted through that work's discursivity—this form of queer theory works as literature. Friends who work in this register often find their work dismissed as too funny, too bitchy, too gay. Too angry, too political. Too sad, too much. Too dirty.

The queer forms of intimacy that Adrian enabled around his work drew us right into the Gordian knot that binds feminine, reproductive labor to a toxic discourse on love and family. Although gay countercultural spaces make room for nonreproductive modes of being, they make less room for expressing such modes of being within a feminine (soft, watery, maternal) context of nonreproductive (or even antireproductive) domestic care and nurturing. Trans houses are an important, enduring example of intergenerational queer caretaking—historically these spaces and forms of intimacy, cultivated by trans women, sit just at the edge of gay and lesbian life. The queer expression of such gendered modes of relation outside socially sanctioned forms (marriage, child-rearing) is rare and fragilized. Add onto this the gender diversity of Adrian's work—in which Adrian moved across gender positions in performance, staged his work in queer and nonqueer spaces, and received a diversity of people in his one-on-one encounters—and we can begin to appreciate the singularity of Adrian's practice, in terms of its sex/gender politics.

Adrian explored the sharp edges of queer alienation from the love apparatus in *May I Have the Pleasure* (2011). In this performance, a small audience (approximately thirty people at a time) encountered Adrian in an environment designed to mimic "the bitter end of a wedding reception disco." The audience was encouraged to relax into the space. He talked with these participants "about being 49, gay, still single, having never been in a serious committed relationship and the painfulness of the loneliness." Adrian continued, "I was sharing that with people that had such—quite often a really judgmental and negative attitude." At the time we spoke, he felt that this performance cost him. The audience members for this particular performance, he explained, "didn't want to be there but didn't know how to leave the space because they didn't really know the rules of the space, and that was a double-whammy for them. They were [also] angry towards me because I was making them uncomfortable, [making them] look at things that they didn't really want to look at in their lives." Although he had worked with these subjects before, he had done so through his persona Adrienne: "*An Audience with Adrienne* was a similar kind of autobiographical piece [in which I talked] about people and things in my life, but I always had the persona, the mask, of Adrienne to perform the autobiographical stories with. But with this piece it [was] without any sort of persona, and actually, all that judgement and negativity and *then* press criticism would actually . . . " At this point there was a brief pause before he named his experience of that paralyzing collapse of work and self, of public and private selves. What was at stake, he said, was "me and my life, it wasn't the show or the material of a show, it was me and my life." He continued, with difficulty, "It really, really wounded me, and it really hurt me and I know that's because the last five years have been a cumulative effect of me being exhausted and running on empty."

Many of us in the auditorium looked at each other. A lot of his peers were there. Many were defining figures in performance. The endless, often humiliating economic struggle of artists is enough, in and of itself, to wear one out. Most of the people in the room do what they do as a matter of survival, however—meaning, there are other struggles that make art making not a luxury, not a lifestyle choice, but a vital necessity.

A few people in the room had brushed up against this awful collapse in which a judgment made against your work becomes a judgment made against you as a person. The most professional of rejections feels like a slap in the face, even when those rejections and criticisms are fair. But the rejection of feminist, queer, and nonwhite artists and writers is often framed by the mischaracterization of our work as propagandistic identity art and as categorically insufficient. Criticism can be mediated by bias and fear, and it is hard to tease out the sting of rejection from the paranoia such criticism breeds among those of us who have felt the freezing wind of exclusion. The "subjectless discourse" of art criticism, at its worst, presents raw sexism, homophobia, racism, and classism as a treatise on, for example, what really counts as contemporary art.

This lining up of your work, your body, and your personal life can be experienced as a violent negation of your dignity and worth. This is, actually, how sexism, homophobia, and racism work. Your body is a problem, an insurmountable symptom of your worthlessness. Your life—your way of living—is a perversion. Your work is an expression of that perversion. Your work is worthless. It takes a lot of emotional strength to rise above all that.

The hours and sometimes days after a performance are strange. The postperformance letdown can be debilitating and disorienting. Even when you know everything went well, as often as not you feel a certain abjection and despair in the event's wake—not because it is over, but because something was let loose.

Adrian spoke very explicitly about this problem. He reminded us that how work feels personal for an artist and for that artist's audience or reader is not symmetrical. One does not mirror the other's feelings.[11] It is not quite right, even, to say that the feelings of artist and audience are mediated by the work of art. More nearly, one encounters the traces or consequences of the other's (absent) presence. Sometimes, those traces and effects are familiar, but sometimes they are alien, and totally unanticipated. We discover those traces as we feel them: there is no knowing the other's feelings. Only the feeling of the other, the sense of another's presence. We know each other by knowing the shape of the distances between us.

We tend to privilege the live encounter in our thinking about questions of presence and proximity. Each medium has its own intimacies, however; each has its way of giving the space between us a form through which we can know it. "Writing," Roland Barthes explains, "is the destruction of every voice, of every point of origin. Writing is that neutral, composite, oblique space where our subject slips away, the negative where all identity is lost, starting with the very identity of the body writing."[12] These lines are from a philosopher who threw himself into his writing with such force that his work is as singular as Roland Barthes was, as a person ("the body writing"). His embrace of the negative space of writing was, for him at least, liberating.

"Whoever you are," Walt Whitman writes, "holding me now in hand, / Without one thing all will be useless, / I give you fair warning before you attempt me further, / I am not what you supposed, but far different."[13] The *me* of those lines is not quite Whitman, but *Leaves of Grass*, the volume of poetry Whitman wrote and rewrote over the arc of his life. He made *Leaves of Grass* to be touched and handled by the reader. *Leaves of Grass* was and is Walt Whitman. He is poetry, but only because he is also not: "I am not what you supposed, but far different." One might want to claim for writing a kind of dominion over this conjuring of the absent presence; absence structures all forms of representation and, in fact, all modes of address, including those which Adrian explored in his work.

Julia Kristeva described the artist as "melancholy's most intimate witness and the fiercest fighter against the symbolic abdication enveloping him."[14] Her influential writing on melancholia (*Black Sun*) is anchored by her curiosity about the nature of the artist's intimacy with despair.[15] In a profound depression, one can be submerged by a thick atmosphere from which language has been exiled. The desire to speak recedes with all other forms of desire ("I am sick to death of the sound of my own voice"). Within this situation—a situation that must but cannot be explained—speaking and writing may not be just painful. Sometimes, it is impossible.

For some psychoanalysts, depression is a nearly primordial state. At its core is an inability to disavow the kernel of despair in all meaning. "There is no meaning," Kristeva writes, "aside from despair."[16] All symbolic forms—all forms of expression—are empty. There is nothing in, nothing to our words in and of themselves. Within this space of such awareness—an awareness of the void—Kristeva writes, "sorrow can be the most archaic expression of a narcissistic wound, impossible to symbolize or name, and too precious for any exterior agent (subject or object) to be correlated to it."[17]

Our words carry meaning only within a social universe held together by the disavowed knowledge of this void, the void internal to the word but also the void into which our words spill. Language is oriented by lack; it is precipitated in us by our separation from "mother," let us say, as a symbolic space. (That zone of feminine care, reproductive labor, and devotion, from which we are all, initially and eventually, expelled, was one to which Adrian was profoundly dedicated.) Language emerges as a means for navigating one's separation, one's expulsion from a state in which there was no other—from a state in which there is no need for language, because one was absorbed in a state of total communion. There is no self, in fact, in such a union. And, in a very real way, that union is beyond our capacity to know and think it; we conjure it in a dream composed from the flotsam and jetsam of what we can know.

Language emerges with the self, with being. The self is never a being in and of itself, outside meaning and language—which is to say, outside despair. Language bridges. All kinds of languages do this, including the language of a man's body lifting its weight off you with the ball of his left foot. We unfold with each other in a constant navigation of, and bargaining with, the annihilating threat of alienation. Language carves out limits—these are not carved in wood or stone, but from the air. These limits are like skin: they define our edges, but they also allow for touch, for experiences of connection, shared sensation, and understanding. The self flows through the world as a mobile, fluid state of interlocking fictions. Kristeva writes,

> Rather than seeking the meaning of despair (which is evident or metaphysical), let us acknowledge that there is no meaning aside from despair. The child-king becomes irremediably sad before uttering his first words. It is being separated from his mother, despairingly, with no going back, that prompts his attempts to recuperate her, along with other objects, in his imagination and, later, in words. The semiology interested in the degree zero of symbolism is unfailingly led to pose questions to itself not only about the amorous state but also about its sombre corollary—melancholy. This entails recognizing, in the same movement, that no writing exists that is not amorous, nor can there be an imagination that is not, manifestly or secretly, melancholic.[18]

If love and melancholia have a primary importance for the artist, this is, for Kristeva, because the drive to make forms—to play with language, sound, images, social rituals, and habits—expresses an openness to spending time in the moment of recognizing that there is no going back. The disavowal available to the nondepressive subject is not exactly a forgetting of this sense of total, irreversible loss but a means of living with it, of internalizing and externalizing the problem of meaning, and of being in relation to each other—one must be able to play with this: "As a lay discourse creating and dissolving the transferential bond, psychoanalysis is an apprenticeship in living beyond despair. It offers not a manic defense against it, but rather a receptivity to it—a way of endowing despair with meaning. By consolidating it in the same way, artistic creation allows the ego to assume an existence on the basis of its very vulnerability to the other."[19] In this functional if not always happy state, we make that leap of faith enabled by knowing that our language may not be full—it cannot carry the full and total sense of our being—but it is full enough (to invoke the vocabulary of Melanie Klein and her "good enough" mother).

Teachers who work with student writing encounter a version of the disabling situation that Kristeva describes and a version of the creative challenge that Adrian described. We encounter young writers unable to disavow their awareness of the intimate relationship between meaning and despair, the knowledge of Nothing. This learning writer can be paralyzed by a sense of their own inadequacy. No sentence is good enough. Their sentences fill them with lacerating self-hatred. These students can't write; a distorted perspective on the abjection of their own writing hobbles them. And yet, sometimes (often?), these students are the Writers—the kinds of writers who write because the activity of writing allows them to keep company with this cosmic despair, to tame it even, or almost. But this is a terrifying business. Perhaps all the more so because the entire situation—the depressive artist, stewing in his (always *his*) own misery—is itself such an awful cliché, cemented in a romantic tradition that exalts some psychic struggles as heroic and denigrates others as weak and self-indulgent. So, the depressive creative subject who can't create (who can't speak, can't write) is burdened with a failure—the embarrassment of having a wrong form of melancholia, being the wrong kind of depressed.

This writing is not just about my conversation with Adrian: it is also about a sequence of losses that have stayed with me. My relationship to my ex, the one to whom I wrote all those love letters, was swallowed up by what looked, to me, like a severe, totalizing depression. When it came for him, he went to bed and stayed there for days, not speaking, not eating. It frightened me in a way that was not helpful for him. This kind of despair is not unfamiliar to me—it's come for my mother (there were times in my childhood when it seemed like she never got out of bed), and it took the life of a friend.

Brian committed suicide in 1997; we were in graduate school together. Our circle was close. He was beautiful, wickedly smart, erudite, hilarious, and an original thinker. He had some very sharp edges, which made him all the more charismatic. We often cooked together, bonding over our shared love for Julia Child and M. F. K. Fisher. I knew he struggled with depression, but he hid the worst of it from most of his friends.

In graduate school, Brian was José Muñoz's very closest friend. I met them both on the same night, at a bar, with a group of people who would become my closest friends. I fell in love with all of them. José writes about Brian's death, or, really, his own grief, in his book *Cruising Utopia*: "I recall all the dreams I have had about him, still have about him, in which he is mysteriously still alive and living in the walls of my apartment. I discover his lingering presence in this recurring dream, and I somehow know that it is my job to get him out, to save him. I never do. I always fail."[20] José was the first of us to get a job and move away from Durham, where we had been students together. He and Brian lived in the same building. They were as close as two people could be. Where José moved through his work very quickly, Brian moved slowly. In those days, graduate programs were not as careful about situations like his: he was not advancing in his degree, but he was teaching for the campus and registering, year after year, as a continuing student. When he died, his community was shaken by grief, guilt, shame, and anger. All of those feelings, for me, clustered around the story the school paper printed about his death.

That article shared details from the police report, telling the story of how he died for a community of readers that included Brian's students. That same article included a quote from a dean that reduced Brian to someone who had not made progress in his dissertation. ("[He] was not registered at the University for the fall semester, said Associate Dean of the Graduate School Leigh Deneef. Although [he] had been in the department for a number of years, Deneef continued, he had not yet finished his preliminary examinations nor formed a dissertation committee."[21]) Even now, I put those sentences in a form of enclosure to bracket off the effects of those words.

The pink program for Brian's memorial has been pinned to the bulletin board above my desk for more than twenty years. Digging around the campus paper's archive, I find a letter that I wrote the paper's editor, one of a group sent to the paper by his friends:

> Though I am shaking with grief at the news of Brian's death, I must respond to your story about Brian Selsky, which appeared in the Oct. 17 edition of The Chronicle. The article was deeply offensive and cruel. The pointless and hurtful reporting of the details of his suicide and the failure on the part of the reporter to contact his students, colleagues or friends for comments on how much he meant to us were stunningly insensitive to say the least.
>
> It is hard not to read your story as indicative of undergraduate and administrative indifference toward the University's graduate students. I knew no one who worked harder than Brian to make the University an ex-

citing, challenging, and interesting place—despite his own ambivalence about the institution.[22]

There is so much in those five sentences. Today, when I read the article reporting Brian's death, I see a student working with genre, much as my own letter inhabits the genre of grievance. The article includes incidental details from the police report that do no more than lend the story the character of crime. A forensic frame gives everything a grim intensity—one powers through details without holding any of them, really. That is something that only the writer or reader who did not know Brian personally can do. Those of us who did know Brian understood every forensic detail too well, and they all hurt.

Today I know that when the press contacts university offices looking for something to put into a story about the death of a member of the campus community, things like this happen. Someone looks up the nature of that person's affiliation, and if that affiliation is worn out, weak, broken, the institutional discourse on their death will map the distance between that person and the institution's sense of its community.

For years after his death, I caught phantom glimpses of Brian at the edges of my vision and in my dreams. José died in 2013: I've never had the experience of thinking I saw my friend out of the corner of my eye, and I only dreamed of José once. In that dream, he is in his tiny New York kitchen, using his Nespresso machine to make me a coffee. He is saying, "You have to try this." Even though I can see José in the dream, I am actually on the other side of the wall—the same wall I've always imagined as the one that appeared in José's dream, the wall that held José's feelings about Brian.

The problem of mourning is an old one for LGBTQ people; a phobic public shames people to death, sometimes with disapproving solemnity, other times with maniacal fury. "Seldom has a society so savaged people during their hour of loss," Douglas Crimp wrote from the midst of the AIDS crisis. "The violence we encounter is relentless, the violence of silence and omission almost as impossible to endure as the violence of unleashed hatred and outright murder."[23] Much of queer theory's initial momentum was derived from the need to describe the compound forms of grief specific to the AIDS crisis, in which one experienced an acceleration and accumulation of loss, as well as a prohibition against acknowledging that loss and, furthermore, a grief at the loss of the forms of experimental sexual community that defined the 1970s and that were fragilized, if not destroyed, by the mid-1990s. "Alongside the dismal toll of death," Crimp writes, "what many of us have lost is a culture of sexual possibility."[24]

Sex changed. Sex changes and drifts; it recedes from us and returns. But, in this essay, Crimp describes the lining up of death with the transformation of a specific community's sense of not just sexual possibility but being possible. AIDS amplifies, condenses, accelerates a problem that was already there. That already-there problem conditions loss.

The word *queer*, for me, works best when it describes a resistance to certain modes of relation, to the sense of property—when it expresses a combative relationship to law and to family, a way of living that makes it very hard to think about one's life as an estate. Death catches us before the distances between our lives and the law have been acknowledged and mapped. Without a will, families take over the work of your friend's burial. There is nothing quite like it—spending those first weeks so grief-stricken, wanting to help, unsure if one should push—watching the family claim a friend's body, as if they were taking it back. This is what happened when José died.

What were we to each other? What are we to each other? What claim do we have on each other's bodies? On each other's deaths? Different communities live with this problem—certain deaths, the deaths that are not the good deaths (at home, surrounded by loved ones, peaceful deaths), leave behind confusion and debris. Slow deaths become quick. We grieve outside institutional structures because our losses are too easily folded into institutional folklore about our foolishness, our failures, our recklessness, our naivete.

I drift back to my lover and the slow-moving hurricane of darkness that came for him. He reminded me a lot of Brian. My insecurity—not (only) regarding his attachment to me, but regarding his attachment to the world—made things worse. I was not an anchor for him; I was a demand.

Adrian and I talked about these feelings of alignment and nonalignment with others, and what they do to us.

"There is no meaning if meaning is not shared," Nancy writes, "and not because there would be an ultimate or first signification that all beings have in common, but because meaning itself is the sharing of Being."[25] It is not that each being has meaning in itself, nor is it that we have a shared, universal meaning. We are meaning only insofar as we are with one another. The word *with*, in Nancy's writing, holds the world. *I* is unbearable, impossible without it. For Nancy, this is "because not being able to say 'we' is what plunges every 'I,' whether individual or collective, into the insanity where he cannot say 'I' either. To want to say 'we' [and here the resonance with Adrian's work is especially powerful] is not at all sentimental, not at all familial or 'communitarian.' It is existence reclaiming its due or its condition: coexistence."[26] If it feels like a lot to frame Adrian's work in relation to existential questions, it is because his work was so touchy-feely, so closely aligned with feminist, antiheroic modes of creative expression dedicated to engaging the ways that we connect with, and rely upon, each other.

This is what our conversation was about. Not how to be, but how to be *with*. When asked if he might protect himself from postperformance exhaustion by drawing stronger boundaries around his performance-self and his self-out-of-performance, he explained:

> I find it really difficult to have boundaries. People ask me if I have particular rituals or whatever in place, either before or at the end of the one-on-ones, for example, and I don't. People have told me about things like wiping myself, wiping my arms or my legs with my hands in the way of wiping off negative energy, and stuff like that, and I just can't really compute that. I just feel that's a really disrespectful thing to do—to wipe somebody's . . . sort of being off of you when you've been holding them.

Being with, in the sense Adrian practiced it, means being responsible to the weight of the other—be that weight symbolic, affective, or material. In our conversation Adrian did not cite the one-on-one performance as problems—not in the sense he describes above, in which it is the weight of the other that bears down on him. The particular postperformance letdown that he was working through at that moment was, he said, specific to the more theatrical performances in which he was, perhaps, asked to perform "being for" rather than "with"; in this context, he had extended himself into the situation of forced social intimacy, meaning, the forced sense of community produced through marriage—a rite that settles who you are really with, once and for all. Those rites of belonging are, indeed, very lonely making. A gay man, staging his isolation and sense of sexual/romantic abjection within the ruin of a wedding reception, was too much for a resistant audience that felt trapped by the whole affair. And it was too much for the artist, triply framed by his own performance, a misalignment between the audience's expectations and needs, and the shape of the actual encounter (surprisingly more participatory than theatrical, in just the way that weddings are).

When Adrian spoke about the shape of the postperformance letdown for the "one-on-ones," the problem was, largely, the scale of his own need as it emerged in that performance's wake. He held because he needed to be held, he cared because he needed to be cared for. He thought with and through that situation.

Adrian said that a spiritual part of himself was held by his audience when they embraced him. He invited people to curl up with him, or to sit in his lap, to give him their weight and be held. He nurtured corporeal exchanges between himself and his audience partners in which they might share the sensation of holding and being held rather than, for example, seeing and being seen. A person who toes the ground to share some of the burden of their weight shares with Adrian a story about their experience of themselves, as does Adrian as he accepts and keeps company with this balletic gesture. A person who curls up in his lap like a cat reveals themselves to him, and he shows them something about himself in the way he receives them. Those performances yield a basic encounter with one's own vulnerability—why would we think they didn't do this for the artist, or that they shouldn't?

2

A PAIN IN
THE NECK

I knew N as a quiet, smart, thoughtful student.[1] I was a member of her dissertation committee and supervised her reading in queer theory. In the spring of 2009, I taught one of my department's large lectures. I asked that she be one of my four teaching assistants (TAs). Months later, she began stalking me.

Looking back, I can see the signs. When she worked for me, she started adding sentimental flourishes to her emails. She also tended to reply to emails I sent to the class team as if they had been written just to her. At the time, these things seemed minor. I pointed them out; I told her to keep the focus of our exchanges on her work. I added the other TAs back into our email chains. She would apologize. And then she'd send me an email because a song made her think of me.

I've heard this kind of behavior described as "intimacy seeking." Sometimes students want to feel a personal connection to you, as a teacher. They may be overly familiar; they might sexualize their attachment to you, or assert a kind of special claim on you over and against all other students.

It is normal for people who have just moved out of their family homes to explore and experiment with the forms of intimacy, belonging, and authority that characterize the campus. The fact that a student might cross a line in email correspondence or even in their behavior toward you does not, in and of itself, constitute harassment.[2] It is the teacher's responsibility to respond to those forms of intimacy seeking by setting limits and showing the student the worth, durability, and value of pedagogical work. Student and teacher collaborate in making that work possible by respecting the boundaries they lay down for each other. It is the teacher's responsibility, however, to take the lead in the work of establishing boundaries with students. That said, this is a joint effort: students who do not respect boundaries set by their teachers can make teaching impossible.

What happened between me and N was truly unusual and made worse by the fact that I'd had no experience with anything like it. Most of the time, graduate students understand pedagogical boundaries before they start their PhD work. But sometimes they don't. Graduate students work directly and intensively with faculty: unless they went to a well-resourced small liberal arts college identified with this kind of personal attention, this mode of collaborative learning will be new to them. The relationship between a graduate student and advisor can feel familial and even, for some, romantic. Being a graduate student is intense. Working with graduate students is intense.

I experience boundaries in graduate pedagogy as an active, ongoing site of negotiation. I struggle with the sense that I do not do enough for my students. Many of us who work in large, underresourced public universities share this feeling. It is not unrelated to anxieties I carried as a student. When I was in graduate school, my insecurity tended to override the support and encouragement I received—I found it hard to believe that my professors would, for example, feel they could never do enough for me. I went into therapy to confront this problem, which, among other things, expressed and reconfigured a conflict between a desire for distance and a need to feel special. Being a good teacher requires that you work that kind of thing out, and not on your students. That is hard work.

There are plenty of faculty who seek intimacy from their students—forms of intimacy that depend on the student's subordination. There are teachers who mirror and amplify the intimacy-seeking gestures that their students make toward them. There are teachers who exploit a student's need to feel special. Some professors do not know how to express attachment and care without sexualizing that relationship. There are teachers who humiliate one student to groom and control another. Some teachers need to feel like the only teacher for their only student—they need to be the teacher who is better, more powerful, more effective, more loving than all the rest. In cases like this, the student's welfare is subordinated to the never-ending project of patching up holes in the professor's ego. Students can collect around these people. One can hardly blame them: the profession rewards sneering bullies often enough.

I sometimes say my case was unusual, but what is a usual case of stalking? In 2009, when this began, I was a regular guest on a local radio program. I was brought in to talk about soccer politics in Los Angeles — I had been blogging about the sport for a few years. My voice, as a sports critic, is quirky and feminist. In one episode, I shared a recurring dream that I'd had been having about being in a three-way relationship with David and Victoria ("Posh Spice") Beckham. In the dream, I was hanging out at their Malibu mansion. We were getting ready to go out to a party. As we went to leave the house, they turned to me and told me I had to stay home — David Beckham said, "We aren't ready to go public with our relationship." He was gentle but firm. I told this story and had a good laugh with the show's host as we speculated about the dream's meaning. (Among other things, there's that need for distance and the desire to feel special!)

The next day, someone posted a flirtatious comment on my sports blog. I deleted the comment and reminded readers to keep their remarks on topic. Then this person emailed my personal account. They did not sign their name, and their email address gave no indication of the sender's identity. Given their use of my still-new personal email address, I was sure it was someone I knew. It was creepy. I told them I would not correspond with them unless they identified themselves. After I made this clear, they seemed to drop the attempt to be in correspondence. However, about three weeks later, they sent an email which suggested that they had been stewing over it:

AUGUST 15

I'm an ally, not an enemy. I try to communicate with you and you take everything the wrong way like I'm a big pervert trying to take advantage of the situation. Why must you take a compliment like an insult? Sounded and looked great on Arellano's show (I presume anyway)!

—A

I did not reply. I was disturbed by the suggestion that they'd seen me at the radio station ("sounded and looked great"), but I didn't dwell on it. I didn't get another anonymous email for months.

That exchange happened at a difficult time in my life. I was a few months out from a devastating breakup. S lived in Germany. It had been a long-distance love affair; we spent time together when we could, but most of our intimacy unfolded over email and via messaging platforms. I had been using my work email for the first few weeks of our relationship. I created my personal email account for our correspondence. Nearly a year into our relationship, he ghosted me. So, at the time, I didn't pay much attention to the anonymous emails. They felt random, and I was grieving the end of a relationship that mattered a lot to me.

Then something creepy happened—something that involved him. I was working on an exhibition and was in that gallery a lot. Unbeknownst to me, a woman working there had dated my ex. One day, she told me this—it was really out of the blue. She told me he'd recently gotten in touch with her. She told me that they were instant messaging while she was working at the gallery and while I was there. She told me that he was still in love with me.

I was so shocked when she said this, I thought I might cry. He wasn't talking to me—but he was Skyping this woman, knowing she was working with me, while I was in the gallery? And he was giving her the impression that he was in love with me? It was such a coincidence that she and I were working together—we were total strangers. I was upset and confused.

I went home, and remembered the comment posted to my blog and those anonymous emails—it hadn't occurred to me that they were from him, but that exchange with the woman in the gallery made me wonder, even, perhaps, hope. So, I messaged him to find out what was going on. I was on edge; he was hostile, and clearly had no idea what I was talking about. I think we told each other to fuck off. I was embarrassed by my wish. I forgot about the emails.

During this period, I was director of our graduate program. A lot was going on at work—things that put the challenges of my personal life in perspective. Over the previous academic year (2008–9) three colleagues died—one, Lindon Barrett, was murdered, and another, Emory Elliott, died suddenly of a heart attack. Another faculty member, Greg Bredbeck, had died the year before—Greg's death was connected to his HIV status and struggles with addiction. (People talk about my department as a great place for queer faculty; is it really though?) Our campus was also rolling with the punches of the economic crisis. We were struggling; my job, as graduate director, required that I be present to graduate students in a time of crisis. I was confronted with quite serious cases of intimate partner violence from within our graduate community. Those stories are not mine to tell, but at least one student's situation makes the story I am telling here seem minor. The terrible handling of those cases by the school shaped my own history.

Looking for relief from my own heartache, I embraced the day-to-day demands of my responsibilities and ignored the warning signs. In the spring of 2009, while N was working as a TA on my class, she organized a campaign to nominate me for a teaching award. I did not like the idea—I was a good teacher, but I was not the kind of dedicated, innovative pedagogue who earns those kinds of awards. I did not fight her too hard, however. While her impulse to nominate me made me uneasy, I didn't want to be an asshole. She got a handful of students to help write and sign the nominating letter, which she showed me.

I caught a glimpse of myself as the sort of professor that students giggle over. It made me uncomfortable. Thankfully, I didn't get the award. Not long afterward, N's emails began to lean into romantic language. Every few weeks, over several months, she would test the boundary of the appropriate, and I would push back. When she signed an email with "regards and kisses," I asked her to come to my office.

I told her (again) that she needed to respect the nature our relationship as student and teacher. I pointed to my own teachers and explained that these were enduring, even lifelong mentoring relationships. I said something about how much Eve Kosofsky Sedgwick had meant to me, that she was a teacher and mentor and that this was a specific kind of friendship, one that required specific and strong boundaries. I told her that, in being her teacher, I was making a commitment to her as a scholar and as a person. But that I could not keep doing so if she continued behaving this way.

She looked me right in the face and said that, because my position prohibited it, I was not expressing my true feelings. She said this as if she knew my own mind better than I ever could. She was very sure of herself, and also very calm.

I was appalled and angry. Not in the habit of yelling at students, I stood up to signal that the meeting was over and asked her to leave my office. I should have resigned from her dissertation committee that afternoon. At the time, I have to remind myself, all that had happened seemed minor. I was worried that my anger at her was out of scale. It was just this attempt to nominate me for an award and romantic language woven into ordinary correspondence and this weird exchange in my office. I could hardly integrate what she'd said—it was so strange, so unexpected. I had not yet put two and two together. Because N and I were in regular communication, and because our interactions were normal, I couldn't imagine that she was behind the anonymous emails I got over the summer.

Just after Valentine's Day in 2010, flowers were delivered to my home. A few dozen short-stemmed roses, accompanied by an unsigned note that said, "to star friendship." It sounded familiar. I googled. The phrase appears in a passage from Friedrich Nietzsche's *The Gay Science*—a text I engage very obliquely in an essay called "Between Friends."

I called the florist. He refused to give me the sender's name. I pushed: they were unwanted, they were creepy. "There is no law that protects the identity of people who send you flowers!" Incredibly, I could not convince him to give me a name, but he did agree to listen to a list of names and confirm who had not sent them. I gave him my ex's name, tried a few other former lovers, and then started naming students. When I got to her, he said nothing. (I phoned that florist several times over months trying to get him to confirm in writing that N sent the flowers, to help me—and he refused!)

I emailed a good friend. I told her about the flowers, the note—I told her that I thought N was likely behind it. "The whole thing just feels wrong," I wrote. Soon after I sent that note, I received this email, from an anonymous sender:

> My darling,
>
> Put down your tomahawk! I sent flowers to make love
> to you, not to start a civil war.
> What does your Friday afternoon look like? Allow me
> to see the plenum of proof in your face and plant
> the new husband's kiss.
> Know that I hold precious and sacred whatever does
> or doesn't happen between us.
> Thinking of you always . . .
> As for my name—I think you know my name already.

A wave of dread washed over me as I read this. I felt sure it was the same person who had emailed me in August and that this person was also N.

I was now anxious that she had access to my email account. I couldn't imagine how N would have known that I was angry about the flowers or that I already suspected her unless she had seen the email I'd sent to my friend.

There was something else. This message also uses distinct phrases drawn from two different poems by Walt Whitman ("plenum of proof" and "new husband's kiss"). I knew those lines; I had used them in correspondence with my ex. I searched my email for those phrases, and there they were—in love letters I had sent to him nearly two years earlier, in 2008. These messages were cut-ups of my own writing—or, more nearly, my own citations. Cut-ups of my cut-ups.

I changed my password.

I googled. First "definition of stalking" and then "what to do if you are being stalked."

I went to the local police precinct and filed a complaint about the flowers and the anonymous emails.

At school, I resigned from her committee. After asking around, I contacted the office that handled sexual harassment cases involving students—the Title IX Office. I filed a complaint—I mapped out N's behavior over the past year and explained that the flowers and anonymous emails were most likely coming from her. When she learned that I had filed a complaint against her, N filed a complaint against me. The school issued an order prohibiting either of us from contacting the other while they conducted their investigation.

At that time, I knew next to nothing about Title IX administration or harassment and stalking. I barely understood why one would need to file a Title IX complaint in a case like mine—I didn't feel discriminated against—I felt stalked.

Things got worse. I started getting calls from blocked numbers and messages from hijacked and spoofed emails. She contacted a friend because she thought their work contained messages from me, to her. She contacted people connected to me because she wanted to get them to pass messages from her, to me. She posted comments to my blog ("It doesn't have to be like this"; "Cunt").

She showed up outside my living room window. One day, I came home from the grocery store to find my front doorstep marked with a fat line of lipstick.

One week, two women students came to see me in my office on different days. In the middle of a normal advising conversation, they said exactly the same thing—as if they had a script: "I really like you." And then, looking right at me, "I'm friends with N." I said something similar to both of them: "I like working with you. You are a great student." I didn't address their reference to N; I hardly knew what to make of that.

Later, one of these women showed up at a class I was teaching, even though she had already graduated. She sat in on my lecture and waited to talk with me afterward—I thought she wanted advice about applying to graduate school. We talked briefly, but when I wanted to leave, the conversation took a bizarre turn. She said, out of nowhere, "I hope you don't think I'm a monster." I told her I could never think that; I expressed concern. But I also felt like I needed to extract myself; something about her demeanor made me afraid she was going to follow me to my car. I felt weird for thinking this, but I managed to get rid of her. I made a very clear pivot, and said something like, "I am walking this way. Take care of yourself. Goodbye."

The other student sent me an email with a link to a piece by a performance artist whose work I had referenced in a lecture. The link took me to an article about a sexually explicit performance by the artist Santiago Sierra, in which he had dozens of people have intercourse.

Although I had referred briefly to other work by this artist in the large lecture course the previous spring, the work I had mentioned was not sexual. This sex-centered work had nothing to do with the class she was taking with me that term; it was relatively obscure. The article, furthermore, was on some kind of alt porn site. The email had a heading like "you don't seem squeamish about sex."

I wrote to the people handling my case at the Office of Student Conduct and at the Title IX Office. Something is going on, I said. Students just do not make these kinds of declarations ("I really like you") or send links to professors that take them to porn sites. "Can you talk to them?"

No one spoke to them.

So much was happening on my end, I didn't follow up with the Office of Student Conduct, but I did talk to the student who was still in my classes. I told her that I had filed a complaint against N. I was apologetic; I knew they were friends. I didn't want her to worry about me, but I was worried that N might have been manipulating her. I felt uncomfortable describing myself (her teacher) as a victim, but I did want her to know that N's behavior was worrying, and I was concerned N might be trying to involve her in her stalking behavior. I encouraged her to speak to the staff handling the case and to a counselor.

While the investigation unfolded at school, I was at the local police station every few weeks writing out odd reports (e.g., "Someone sent me flowers with a creepy quote from Nietzsche." "Someone marked my doorstep with lipstick."). Each incident was so small; it felt silly that I was, by this point, so unnerved. But guidelines for stalking victims suggest filing these reports in order to establish a record, in case things get worse. At some point my reports crossed a stalking threshold, and my case was assigned to the Los Angeles Threat Management Unit (TMU). They called me in for an interview.

This office describes itself as the world's first policing unit dedicated to stalking, and as the world's best. Their job, as they described it to me, was to convince N to stop stalking me and to, in doing so, keep her from ending up in jail. Their work began with a risk assessment. I drove to their headquarters—a sharp, gleaming concrete, steel, and glass complex in downtown Los Angeles. When I went there in 2010, the building was new to the city. Today, this striking building features prominently in the Amazon series *Bosch*; it is the architectural manifestation of the LAPD's management of its own capacities for violence and care. It feels more corporate than cop.

The detectives led me through glass doors, onto their open-plan floor. As I walked in, I noticed a framed photograph on the opposite wall. It was a portrait of Rebecca Schaeffer, the popular, lovable star of the CBS sitcom *My Sister Sam*. On July 18, 1989, she was shot on the doorstep of her home by Robert Bardo. He stalked her for three years before he killed her. He paid a detective $250 to get her home address from the Department of Motor Vehicles. The first antistalking laws were passed in the wake of her death. Bardo was given a life sentence; he was prosecuted by Marcia Clark, who would later prosecute O. J. Simpson. Of this case, a forensic psychiatrist observed that "hate mail isn't as dangerous a sign as obsessive love mail."[3]

Two TMU detectives interviewed me in a room just like the ones you see on TV. They began with four questions. Is she smart? (Yes.) Does she have a drug problem? (Not that I know of.) Did she have unsupervised access to any of your computers? (Maybe.) Does she have a gun? (I don't know.) The first question (Is she smart?) surprised me; I asked them to explain.

From a policing perspective, they said, self-identified smart people can be scary. They are not inhibited either by the law (because they believe they can work around it) or by the problem of not knowing how to do something (because they are good at teaching themselves what they don't know). This sounded familiar: the academy is filled with people who think they are the smartest people in the room.

In the interview, they spent some time exploring how each of these incidents made me feel. They told me to get rid of any computers she might have accessed. It requires a lot of expertise (and money) to find malware, and some forms of it can't be removed from a computer, even if you replace the hard drive. We would never know, in other words, if she'd accessed my computers.

They said that getting rid of my computers was a concrete action that would give me peace of mind. I didn't need to know if or prove that she had access to my computers, they explained, I needed to know that she didn't. Replacing my desktop and laptop, they said, was far more effective than trying to demonstrate if she had done something like this. It was something I could do to reestablish a sense of digital privacy, at least in relation to her. In general, they taught me to look for the thing I could do in the here and now, independent from school or the police, to feel safer.

Digital media is a hothouse for harassment and for paranoia. It takes relatively little to reach into a person's world to make them feel surveilled within platforms that are themselves data vacuums. One hardly need put malware on someone's computer to reach into their digital space. If she did once have access to my email account, it would almost certainly have been because I had a very simple password, which she saw me type out. I doubted that she'd have put malware on my computer. And, by this point, I was not sure where she'd found the Whitman—the lines she quoted were particularly significant to me because I had sent them to S. But for that same reason, I had written on a blog about both of the poems from which those lines were drawn. She might have just had a keen eye for phrases that mattered to me.

I often cycle like this. When I feel overwhelmed by the sense that she infiltrated my private life, I talk myself down, dismissing the reasonableness of the anxiety. I shove aside the reason why I felt sure she gained access to my email. Not long after she sent me those flowers, as I tried to find evidence linking her to the anonymous emails and the flowers, I read a blog she once told me she had been writing—a blog loosely associated with the reading she was doing as a part of her dissertation research. One entry featured three photographs of her in a white sleeveless undershirt, posing for the camera. These had no obvious relationship to the blog and were uncannily similar to three photographs of myself I had sent to my ex, attached to an email that included those lines of Whitman's.

The pictures she seemed to be citing were part of an archive of erotic self-portraits I'd produced for my ex. I was wearing a shirt he'd left at my house; a shirt I still have because, of course, this is not just any ex. At the time, he was the last person I'd fallen in love with, and he really broke my heart. Those photographs of my student mimicking me in love were horrifying. (Could this really have been a coincidence? Was I projecting this fear/fantasy?) When I met with the detectives, I had a printout—screenshots taken of her blog and screenshots of the emails I had sent to my ex. This is why there was a sense of urgency to the need to reestablish a sense of boundaries in my digital world. Those exchanges with S are the only sustained erotic correspondence I have ever allowed myself. I am not ashamed of them, but I can't imagine ever enjoying that again—not because our relationship was such a disaster, but because that archive was contaminated by the stalking.

I did what the detectives told me to do. I swapped out my devices. I was surprised by how much this did for my peace of mind.

In our work together, the detectives said we had to address my fear and prioritize ending the stalking above all else. They would work to make sure she understood the risks she was taking with her own life by giving in to her impulses. And they kept me out of that process.

Talking to these detectives made me feel better; they told me they often handled cases like mine and that a lot of their victims were school employees or students. They made me feel better, not only because they helped me prioritize my well-being; they left me feeling that they wanted to make sure things didn't get worse for N. The problem, in other words, wasn't N. It was the stalking dynamic itself.

These detectives worked for the LAPD. I was incredibly ambivalent about going to the police about N's behavior. She'd been outside my house, her behavior was escalating, and I was feeling threatened. I was very lucky. Most do not have access to people who have this kind of training in stalking. My case, furthermore, was routed into a diversion program intended to minimize escalation and keep people out of prison. The detectives told me that they work with a lot of teachers, especially for the kind of stalking I was enduring— meaning, intrusive behavior characterized by delusion.

I asked the people handling my case at school to talk to the detectives handling my case. I tried to explain: they had ideas for de-escalation and also for increasing our collective safety. The people handling the case at school refused to do this—not out of any abolitionist leanings but, I think, out of a commitment to the policing logics particular to our campus. If anything, the people at school burrowed deeper into their own *Law & Order* fantasies. The university hired a private security firm to consult with my landlord in order to "harden" my apartment. They wanted to fence in the building; guests would need a code to get through the front gate. My landlord was a harassing presence (asking out tenants, lurking outside our apartments, pestering one woman so much she and her husband left)—the last thing any of us wanted was to be locked inside a compound with him!

I told the people at school that I did not want to live in a bunker. I did what a lot of stalking victims do: I moved.

I was so preoccupied by the general weirdness of being stalked that I did not think much about the school's Title IX process. I did not see N's complaint against me until I was interviewed during the school's investigation.[4]

It was very much like an episode of *Law & Order*; it was, actually, more like an episode of *Law & Order* than the risk-assessment interview I had with the LAPD detectives. I was in a windowless room with the two campus investigators. One of them slid the document across the table. I picked it up and read it.

I honestly did not fully appreciate my situation until I read this document. I had assumed N knowingly filed false charges against me. But as I read through the document, I saw something else.

N wrote that there was a "morse code like aspect" to my communications with her. She described a series of instances in which I had done something very ordinary but which she described as an overt sexual demand. When I read the complaint, I felt that her charges were sincere—meaning, it seemed possible to me that the things she was describing were real to her.

All of the incidents she described were rooted in things that had really happened. After lecture, for example, I often asked my TAs to meet me outside the classroom to check in. She charged, however, that I'd whispered in her ear, "I'll wait for you outside." Other charges pointed to my work—to, for example, my 1999 essay on Thomas Eakins. In 1886, he was forced out of his teaching position in what, today, we would call a case of sexual harassment. I was one of the first scholars to take the complaints against him seriously as a framework for thinking about his work. "To my way of thinking," she wrote, "Professor Doyle's research influences not just her writing, but her behavior and actions." She accused me of "engag[ing] in sexual banter" and of wanting "a sexual 'pedagogic' relationship." (In my writing on Eakins, I contest art historical depictions of Eakins as a maverick, situate his behavior as a kind of bullying/harassment, and read his approach to the nude within that context.) N also accused me of greeting her with European-style kisses at an art event I hosted. I do not remember greeting her in this way, but I did greet a lot of people at that event with hugs, handshakes, and kisses on the cheek. She took this as "flirting."

Other charges were stranger. She described standing with me near a coffee kiosk on campus. She described us as in conversation. Then she described herself feeling like I was too close, so she said, firmly, "I'm going this way," and pivoted ninety degrees to walk away, trying to make clear in her body language that she did not want to be followed. I recognized this as a very close description of the choreography of the odd conversation I'd had with the undergraduate I'd spoken to after class—the one who said, "I hope you don't think I'm a monster," and who I was afraid was going to follow me to my car. I wondered, had she been watching us? Had she overheard me describe this encounter to a friend?

I tried to contextualize these charges for the investigator, but I also wondered how they could investigate a series of charges like that. After all, how exactly does one prove that I am not communicating with N in code?

There was one charge that bothered me more than any of the others. She alleged that in a meeting with my TAs, I had complained about neck pain. She accused me of asking her for a neck massage.

I sat there, under the watchful eyes of the investigators, trying to remember—I had a bout of neck pain a year earlier; I had told my TAs about it. I did not ask them for a massage. But something about that one accusation got under my skin.

When I read that charge, in March 2010, it had been a while since I had thought about the week that Eve Kosofsky Sedgwick died.

In early April 2009, a friend called to tell me that Eve, our teacher and friend, was dying. I flew out to keep vigil with my friends from grad school. I stayed with them as long as I could.

On April 13, I flew back to Los Angeles from New York. I had to teach the next day—the big lecture for which N was a TA. When I landed, I learned that Eve had died.

The next morning, I woke up with a severe pain in my neck. When I got to campus, I met my TAs and told them that I was in a lot of pain. I asked them to administer a test later that week, so I could stay home and rest. We talked briefly about Eve's death; I said something about not wanting to talk about it, because I needed to get ready for lecture.

In the afternoon, I made my way over to class. When I came into the lecture hall, N was standing at the front of the room. She was in the middle of announcing to a class of nearly three hundred students that my friend and teacher had died.

I was mortified. It felt very wrong. And then I felt like jerk: Wasn't she just trying to be nice? How could she know that this was very much the opposite of what I wanted or needed? That, as a teacher, I did not want my students feeling sorry for me? And: Eve hadn't been dead twenty-four hours; it was upsetting just to hear it said out loud.

I walked to the front of the classroom and launched myself into my lecture as if nothing had happened; pinned between anger and grief, I closed myself up.

More recently, I remembered something else. Eve was diagnosed with breast cancer in 1991. The cancer came back in her neck in 1996; at that time, I was one of her PhD students and part of her circle. She had radiation treatments that burned her throat so severely that eating was a chore. I helped out by experimenting with recipes for soups and ice cream—I made forms of smooth deliciousness that I thought she could eat, if not with pleasure, then without pain. I felt grateful that she let me do things like that for her.

I felt close to Eve, but I did not think of myself as a member of her innermost circle. I'd been to her house; I'd sat at her dinner table and cooked for her. I was her student, a mentee, who shared a special time with her while she taught at Duke in the 1990s. And, as I had explained to N in that meeting in my office, that relationship was important to me—as important as any other form of kinship and intimacy. Her writing was a crucial model for me: her work could be sexually frank without being sensationalizing. She shared so much in her writing but mobilized the personal in deeply philosophical ways. (Her work was nevertheless received in some quarters as if it were pornographic.) In our relationship as teacher and student, I nested in a space similar to that which she made for me in her writing. Close but not too close. I think of this as an intentional and pedagogical form of closeness.

It is easier for me to articulate all of this now. It was years before I could really mourn Eve, however. When I ask myself to identify the start of the whole stalking story, I think of the moment when I saw N announcing Eve's death to my students, and when I walked down to the front of the lecture hall to teach, as if nothing was wrong.

The complaint I filed at school was supported. The complaint N filed against me was dismissed. At that point, she was presenting her stalking behavior as her dissertation—a turn that won't be too much of a surprise to people who have years of experience as teachers.

My department ended her graduate study at this point; no one on the faculty would work with her. If only things had stopped there—with the set of actions taken by the people who worked most closely with her.

The administrators running the Student Conduct Office decided, however, that they wanted to hold a student conduct hearing in which the question of whether she was harassing me would be decided again. It was scheduled several weeks after she lost her student status. I fought this hearing. What was the Title IX investigation and report for? What if the committee decided that she wasn't stalking me? How could they do this if she was no longer a student? What if this committee decided she was, in school's language for such things, "not responsible"? This new hearing made no sense to me.[5]

I talked to the detectives handling my case. They were clear: this hearing would only make things worse. Ideally, they said, there should be no hearing. If that hearing had to be held, she and I should appear before the committee on separate days. They also said that I should not allow them to record an interview with me and then give that recording to her—that any material like that would be, in essence, fuel for her stalking campaign. They also felt she should not be allowed to ask me questions in that hearing. The material this hearing would produce would become powerful parts of her library—this was terrible for de-escalating her stalking, especially given the affective stakes of this hearing, its promise to validate N and her experience of being in relation to me. From the school's perspective, the boundaries I needed were impossible to uphold. It is the right of anyone participating in hearings like this to have access to recorded testimony. And, at that time, my campus allowed victims to be directly examined by the people they accused.

In the weeks leading up to that hearing her behavior grew more and more disturbing. Her behavior was so upsetting that a member of the legal team working my case at school called me at home and told me that N was "disconnected from reality" and that I needed a restraining order. She said that I should go to the LA County Courthouse and file for one right away. I had seen N outside my house the day before; I took what she said seriously—this woman was a lawyer with, I thought, a lot of relevant experience.

I didn't know anything about restraining orders. I spent the day in the courthouse learning the hard way. In Los Angeles, there is a specific room in the courthouse dedicated to processing petitions for restraining orders filed by family members and partners against their loved ones—the day I went to the courthouse, that room was filled with women of color, many of whom had children on their laps.

If you are in a room like this, your fear for yourself and your loved ones has overridden your fear of the police, even given what you know about them. I was sent to a different place—this was more like an office, and they seemed to handle every other form of restraining order.

At that time, in California, you couldn't win a restraining order without solid evidence of a direct threat. By the time I filed my paperwork with a judge, I felt confident that my petition would fail. N sent me very love-and-deathy messages. They were very creepy. For example, on the day she marked my doorstep with lipstick, she posted the following on her blog: "Imagining a chocolate brown nipple in my mouth and a tidy athletic A-cup in my hand. Yum. P.S. I fucking hate you. . . . And I always leave a calling card. The details. It's always in the details." This is not directly threatening. This material was directed at me, but it was not sent to me. It appeared in a personal blog post almost certainly read by no one but me, but that is not at all the same as an email sent to me. Even a blog post of a picture of a gun (positioned next to a painting I'd written about—Édouard Manet's *Olympia*) was not a direct enough threat, especially given that it was captioned by "ceci n'est pas un pistolet." She often referenced texts I'd written about, or to which I'd referred in class or in conversation—texts in which characters die. *Hamlet*, *House of Mirth*, *Fight Club*. This was not enough to restrict her civil liberties. By the time I filled out the forms, I didn't know what I wanted.

The judge denied my petition and said that it was a matter for the school to deal with. I went home in tears, because, of course, it had been the person handling things at school who had sent me to court. It would be months before I learned that state and federal workplace violence prevention law required the school to support me. That is what the judge had meant. There is a particular kind of restraining order for workplace situations: it is filed not by the victim, but by their employer. This was, at the time, particularly important, because once she lost her status as a student, she was not subject to any rules from the campus regarding coming onto campus or contacting me or my colleagues.

I felt angry, manipulated. I struggled with my own lack of understanding, and it took me time to get to where I am right now.

People in general can be naive about restraining orders. Restraining orders are offered to victims of relational abuse as an important tool. By the time people start telling you that a temporary or emergency restraining order is necessary, you are desperate for relief from whatever it is you are being subjected to. But who uses this tool? Who enforces a restraining order if not the police? It is a blunt-force administrative tool with a carceral telos.

Although restraining orders can provide a strong boundary, they can also be used by abusers to harass their victims and can contribute to an escalation of risk and a potential for violence. Any legal instrument that creates a situation in which police are called in and people are, by default, hauled off to jail increases the likelihood that someone will be hurt. In 2013, Sam See, a queer man of color and much-loved faculty member at Yale University, died in police custody; he and his husband were caught in an abuse dynamic and had mutual restraining orders against each other. The police were called to an argument between them and arrested them both. Outside his community, the sense of the injustice of See's death faded with the release of a medical report that identified a drug overdose as its cause.[6] See's death, however, was the product of the procedural instruments of carceral culture. There are no easy answers to abuse/harassment dynamics: de-escalation requires specific training, the capacity to understand an abusive dynamic, and collaboration within and between communities. But we can say with absolute certainty that jails and prisons are instruments of enormous violence and make things worse. This is why I say that we were lucky my petition was denied.

When the school scheduled her disciplinary hearing, I talked with the detectives managing my case. They did not recommend being on campus at the same time as N. They felt it was risky. At minimum, the hearing was likely to amplify and intensify her stalking impulses. Every experience I'd had up to this point indicated that this was true. The main issue was her ongoing behavior toward me. I thought my physical presence at the hearing was not necessary because the school had the report from the Title IX investigation. Technically, I wasn't the agent of the hearing at all: it was convened by the Office of Student Conduct. It didn't occur to me that this hearing was about whether or not she stalked me. I assumed that the investigators' report established for a fact that she had. It frankly mystified me that I was being pressured to attend and be questioned by her.

I struggled to understand the behavior of my colleagues at school—everything they did seemed to make things worse, in no small part because they pushed me to do things like apply for restraining orders without a real sense of what they are and what they do. How could the head of the school's investigation phone me to tell me she feared for my safety and then send me to the courthouse alone and with no guidance? The staff at school had direct contact with N; by this point, I did not. How scary was N being? Why didn't they just explain to me what was making them so afraid for me?

The people at school wanted me to get a restraining order to protect myself against her, but they also wanted me to sit in a room with her. They thought I needed a restraining order, but they also wanted to allow her to cross-examine me? They told me that at the hearing, in fact, I would need to explain my teaching philosophy for the committee hearing the case. I was told that I would need to defend myself against the accusation that I "sexualize the classroom," as that was her defense. I was also told "not to get defensive" because that would be "bad."

They had the report from the Title IX investigation, and she was, from my department's perspective, no longer a student, so what did they need me for? What was this hearing's purpose? I was really through. I told the folks at school that if they wanted to hold this hearing, they would have to do it without me. I warned them: She's smart.

The day after the hearing, I was contacted by the woman who had presented the case to the committee. "It's not good." She couldn't tell me what happened, but she said I should brace myself. She also told me the hearing lasted nine and half hours, the longest ever conducted on our campus.

A couple weeks later, I was sent a copy of the memo that summarized the hearing and its outcome: the committee found her "not responsible" for stalking and harassing me. Authored by the chair of the Student Conduct Committee and addressed to N, the memo revealed that during the hearing she had played a recording of me: "You also presented a video to the committee containing footage of the professor conversing with a student about you. You stated that you obtained the video footage and had the video edited to omit the student's voice." This is mentioned as an incidental detail. Although I'd felt watched, until I was shown this memo, I had no idea that she was recording me. The memo said nothing about how, where, or when I'd been recorded. For weeks I didn't know the extent of it, and my imagination roamed wild.

I was told that I wasn't supposed to have seen that memo, and that I should not discuss it with anyone.[7] Then I was told I would never know the names of the colleagues who watched that video and decided she was not stalking me.

I asked for a recording of the hearing. I was told I wasn't allowed to have this. I then insisted on having a copy of those portions of the recording in which I was speaking. I was eventually given a ten-minute excerpt. In that part of the hearing, N played a video. I could hear myself talking—I was talking about N.

I knew the context immediately: I was talking to one of the students who had come to my office and recited that spooky script—"I really like you. [Pause.] I'm friends with N." It was the student who had sent me the link to the porn site; the student I had tried talking to about her friendship with N. Because she was in my class, because she was my student and I didn't want to be alarmist, I minimized the impact of N's behavior on me even as I described N's behavior as crazy. I actually said that I didn't feel harassed, which wasn't true. But those were my words.

I don't know if that's why the committee found her "not responsible" for stalking and harassing me. Even given the fact that I had said "I don't feel harassed" to this student, the fact that I was being secretly recorded at the time by that student, should, I think, have demonstrated beyond any doubt that I was being stalked.

The staff at the Office of Student Conduct appealed the committee's decision to the dean of students, and it was overturned. This was inevitable. The whole hearing was wildly unnecessary if only because N wasn't a student at the time the hearing was held. Graduate students can lose their status on academic grounds, and there are quite different procedures for appealing that form of dismissal. This was another reason I refused to participate: N's status as a student had ended two weeks before the hearing.

This kind of confusion and failure is at the heart of complaints about how schools have handled harassment. As I went through this, I kept thinking, I'm a tenured professor. How much worse is it when the victim is a student and the accused is a faculty member? And I thought about N, too: How was any of this helpful to either of us? But I was truly haunted by the committee's decision.

I came away thinking that if this group of people could not find her responsible for stalking and harassing me, if a committee could discard the findings of a Title IX investigation, it was because a lot of faculty do not believe harassment matters. And that represented, for me, a much deeper problem than N's stalking. No policy is better than the people charged with honoring it.

I was plagued by questions about what else had happened at that hearing, not only because I was worried about what else N was doing that I didn't know about. I was worried about how faculty, colleagues, handled my work. I insisted I be given a copy of the recording of the entire proceedings. I argued that the recording included evidence of ongoing stalking behavior. I also argued that because the committee included colleagues, I had a right to hear those portions of the hearing in which I was the focus of discussion.

I was eventually given a recording of all but the committee's deliberations: it had been burned onto a CD for me. I took it home and listened to all of it. The irony of the whole situation was not lost on me: I hadn't participated in the hearing in part because I had not wanted to produce recorded material that N might then weaponize in her stalking—if I'd been there, she'd have been studying and "decoding" this material much as I was doing.

The hearing opens with a breakdown of the case. After the head of the Title IX office describes the investigation, a man interrupts her to express open contempt for her work. He sounds like senior faculty. He describes his department and himself as "persecuted by Title IX." I took this to mean that he himself had been the object of a complaint. He speaks with sneering contempt about Title IX—he can hardly restrain his disgust with the staff person presenting the case—that disgust seems to extend to the idea of Title IX itself.

After staff finished presenting the case against her, N begins her defense. She brings up the complaint that she filed against me. Staff stop her: "This hearing is not about Dr. Doyle." The same man interrupts them to say that he wants to hear about this complaint against me. He opens the door for N and holds it open.

She stays on the subject of me for hours. She shows them the secretly recorded video of me talking with that student in my office. N talks at length about my romantic life, as she understood it. She talks about my hair. She acts out my mannerisms. N talks about an abortion I had when I was in college (something I referenced in an essay, in a footnote, once)—all this is raised in defense of her stalking behavior.

The student who had recorded me testifies as a witness; that student presents the syllabus for a senior seminar in queer studies, which she had taken. The syllabus is treated as evidence of sexual misconduct. She talks about how one day, a button came loose on my blouse and she'd seen my bra. She says I'd done it deliberately. She talks about the work of other gay students in the class, as if what they did was inappropriate. Men in the class had designed a speculative cruising map for the city, for example, imagining who you might find where. This is treated as evidence of the "sexualization of the classroom." The committee seems to take this seriously.

N talks about a short essay I'd written about *Jude the Obscure*, my writing on *Moby Dick*, my sports blog. The only time a member of the committee interrupts her to question the relevance of the material she is presenting is when she starts to discuss a blog post I'd written about Canada's national women's hockey team.

A few months earlier, N had presented this material to the Title IX investigative team—she gave them citations from my articles, material from my book and my sports blog, and fragments of work by other people. It was, I understand, an annotated bibliography of my work and the work of my friends. According to the Title IX Office's report, she argued that this material demonstrated that I was "'covertly communicating' with [her] through public channels." At one point in this process, she presented this material as her dissertation. The investigators dismissed this argument as "bizarre." The faculty on the Student Conduct Committee, however, took it seriously.

Sometimes I wish I'd never been given that recording. My colleagues threw the university's investigative report out the window and credentialized the narrative of a woman who argued I was communicating with her in code. The ultimate problem was the content of my work: my first book is called *Sex Objects: Art and the Dialectics of Desire*, for example.

As I listened, I felt the mirroring of her recording of me in my listening to this recording of her. The most disturbing thing about that recording is not what she said, however. It is that a committee of my colleagues listened to her for hours, watched covertly recorded video, and then cleared her of stalking and harassment. That has never stopped bothering me.

Things changed. Months after the hearing, as the university unlocked its grip on N and as the people managing the case in the district attorney's diversion program took over, the institutional apparatuses holding us in relation to each other fell away. The intensity of N's behavior toward me dissipated. Her messages became far less frequent and less harassing. They gradually lost their unsettling power.

On Valentine's Day, in 2011, I got a strange email: "The mystery of revelation 10;7 must be completed, that is how the rapture is to be properly announced, the mystery of revelation 10;7 must be completed." The next year, flowers were delivered to me at school by the woman who had said she was "a friend of N's," who said, "I hope you don't think I'm a monster." In March 2014, someone wrote a friend, claiming she bought an old computer of mine at a yard sale—she asked that friend to pass her contact information to me so that we could talk. For a while, I got random, urgent requests for copies of my syllabi and emails of lines of verse ("now show me your universe, the whole thing"). Every now and again, handwritten letters appear in my mailbox. Nevertheless, the sense of dread that had flooded my life receded.

Until I sat down and reviewed these old incidents, I thought of them as less disturbing—but in a way they are quite the opposite. They are unhinged, and, assuming they are from her, they are heartbreaking. But they are not dialed into my life. Again, if they are from her, they track the drift of her thinking and feeling away from my life. If they do not bother me, it is because they do not speak to me, or, rather, they do not speak through me. They feel like signals from another cosmos. (If they are not from her, they signal the residual trace of her paranoia in me.)

Over a period of years, I got more and more of my life back and tried to metabolize what I have been through. I started writing about security dynamics, harassment, and Title IX—the work that became *Campus Sex, Campus Security*. That book is not about my case, but it is informed by my experience of ideas, fantasies of persecution and policing, safety and security as they shape our interactions with each other at school. I started following harassment cases in the academy; I started studying them. And then something else happened.

In 2014, just as I was finishing *Campus Sex, Campus Security* and repositioning myself as a scholar working on harassment, paranoia, and institutions, another, much bigger case emerged in my department. Multiple students came forward with harassment complaints against a faculty member. In the very early days of that case, I talked with two of the complainants and helped direct them to people in my department who needed to hear these accusations. I wrote to our chief campus counsel to alert him to what I understood to be very serious charges, and expressed concern about the campus's ability to administer a complaint of this scale.

A lot happened in and around my department over the next few years. My role in that case was limited: mainly, I picked up advisees who had previously been working with him. I was, in that sense, a direct witness to the impact of his behavior on them.

I hadn't fully processed the impact of my own case on my life. I started to appreciate the harm done to me by seeing the harm done to them. Things I'd internalized as personal failings were symptoms. As a teacher, I found this very hard—I felt self-conscious of even my desire to help as a symptom. I did not trust my department or campus when it came to looking out for them; that lack of trust is itself a deep wound.

Soon after students came forward with their charges, the accused faculty member reached out to me. He wanted my support. I did not write back. I knew enough about the case to want nothing to do with his defense. I blocked him on social media. A colleague in my department encouraged me to take up his case. I told them that I knew too much to do something like that, hoping that they respected my work in this area enough to take the hint. Things got weird.

Every few months, over a period of years, he sent email to me. He argued that the victims made up their accusations against him. Sometimes it seemed like he was still hoping I'd become his defender, and sometimes he suggested I had somehow been an agent in his firing. It was an eerie echo of N's posture toward me: solicitous and resentful.

He began trolling me lightly from sockpuppet accounts on Twitter, usually with quotes from Laura Kipnis's book, *Unwanted Advances*. The lines he used were from a paragraph in her book in which she describes his case, from his point of view. He shared some of his own writing about his case. He sometimes made references to mine.

His emails and tweets made me think that he was talking to N. Once, for example, he emailed me a screenshot of one of my tweets. I had posted a link to a news article that I'd appreciated for its reporting. The story featured a name that was identical to my stalker's. The subject line for the email was "harassment trolling? gaslighting." When he sent me that email, the stalking had drifted so far from my life I hadn't noticed that the story included someone with N's (fairly common) family name. I couldn't imagine why he would be reading my social media posts that closely, and then make that link and feel compelled to send me this note, unless he was talking with N.

At about this time, N reached out to someone involved with her case at school (another victim of her stalking behavior), expressing a desire to talk about "2010," the year things got really bad. That person wrote to me to let me know. That same month, my department received a disturbing email that seemed to spin around my writing on harassment.

The same day we got that email, someone posted an even more disturbing comment on an old blog post of mine: it was an awful diatribe about white women and Black men. A friend was staying in my apartment; I wondered if N had figured out where I live and if she had been watching my place. I put that worry aside. A few weeks later, I thought I saw her on the street in front of my place. I had been waiting for a ride. A woman who looked very much like her was approaching me as I got into the car. The driver asked if she was OK. He said she didn't look "right."

I was rattled but talked myself down. Why would she take such a risk? I thought I must have imagined it. And then I thought, there's not much I can do, and it's still not as bad as it was. But I could not shake the feeling that she was in communication with my former colleague—or, at the very least, that my colleague wanted me to think this. The fear I felt about her being outside my apartment alerted me to the fact that this possibility really bothered me.

My former colleague wrote me again: "The following blog post will appear online soon, with many more to follow. Enjoy!" Attached was writing about the people who had filed complaints against him. He'd sent me things like this before; usually these included texts and photographs from exchanges between him and his former students—these screenshots were relatively benign, but sexual in nature.[8] These people were my advisees. I was sick of his attempts to humiliate them and to harass and goad me. I experienced his weaponization of student correspondence with him as a form of revenge porn, and I wasn't having it.

In casual conversation about stalking and harassment, people often say to me that the best tactic is to ignore it. I'd ignored this guy's emails for years. It really didn't matter. The problem was that I existed and that I cared.

I decided that enough was enough and so, drawing from what I'd learned, I wrote him back: "Do not contact me by email or any other means." I wanted to put the unwanted nature of this email on the record. He wrote back three times in quick succession. He sent me tips on using email filters and then let me know that he was, indeed, talking to N.

> Personally, I recommend spam filter. You set it up, my emails go in the trash automatically, presto!
> I know [N] has to do something like that to keep you from harassing her.

I have not responded to an email from N since I filed the complaint against her in 2010. N, however, might experience any text—spam, email, my publications—as a message from me. She might also manipulate this guy to push him to write things like this to me; her way of staying in touch in a world that prohibits any direct communication.

Once I made it clear I didn't want to hear from him, ever, my former colleague picked up the pace; for a few months he wrote to me as if we were in an ongoing toxic conversation. He sent me a link to an article by Laura Kipnis. He wrote, "Wouldn't you kill, to write something this powerful, this relevant, instead of the narcissistic drivel you churn out? It must really eat at you that she will always be smarter and more famous than you are." That message helped me to finally understand his fixation on me. Kipnis wrote about complaints filed against the philosopher Peter Ludlow; she published a high-profile article about them in the *Chronicle of Higher Education*, and then she wrote about the complaints filed against her, braiding her own sense of persecution with his. She then wrote a bestseller. He wanted me to be his Kipnis.

I felt worn down and just wanted him to stop. What is the right thing to do? Direct his emails to trash and hope for the best? Mark each as evidence in case of some future disaster? I posted one of his messages onto my Instagram account, thinking he might stop if he thought that everything he sent me was public. He wrote to tell me that my writing about what happened to me is a form of retaliation against N. He wrote to remind me that a faculty committee found her innocent. He claimed to be working on a story about his case. I decided to write it all down, just in case. That is how this piece of writing came to be.

I adjusted my filters so that anything from my former colleague's email address was archived and forwarded to campus counsel. I shared a summary of his behavior in a department meeting; I wanted my colleagues to share the worries of my situation. I wanted people to understand that this was work. And then he stopped.

Every now and again I meet other stalking victims, and we say things like this to each other:

> Even your own experience as a stalking victim is colonized by the stalker.
>
> They stalk you because they feel like you are stalking them.
>
> They feel persecuted by your mere existence.
>
> Your survival is hitched to someone else waking up from a bad dream.
>
> It feels like you have been evicted from your life by someone who claims it as their rightful belonging.
>
> The place you feel least safe is your own mind.

Stalking victims abandon routines, get PO boxes, stop answering their phones. Stalking victims move from their homes, change jobs, drop out, change names.

These changes, however, are just material. Inside, you abandon whole sections of your being as if you were, yourself, contaminated.

I first shared this narrative in a reading at an art space in Los Angeles in January 2019. I was in an altered state as I told this story to a room full of friends and many of my students. N might have been there. I avoided looking for her in the audience and worked on accepting her as one of my readers. It was a real exercise in letting go.

3

A CASE OF
PARANOIA

I recovered some sense of myself by adopting a forensic curiosity about my situation. I became a harassment scholar, working my way through a growing syllabus of writing about bureaucracies, institutions, risk management, forensic psychiatry, harassment dynamics, and the administration of complaints. My study is idiosyncratic, shaped more by exigencies of circumstance than by discipline. The nature, shape, and problem of paranoia flows through this personal library.

Paranoia has an endless appetite.[1] It is a style of thought (organized and systemic, binarized and projective), a set of feelings (persecutory, excited, frustrated, angry), a position (defensive), a mood (manic, pessimistic, aggressive, dark), and a clinical term describing a specific set of psychological struggles. Paranoia can characterize a person's or a group's relationship to the world—in fact, some have argued that groups are particularly good at paranoia.[2] We are most familiar with its manifestation as a spiraling sensitivity to humiliation and insult that can carry increasing densities of meaning. These insults can assemble into persecutory delusions that range in scale and intensity from a nagging insecurity (my boss really doesn't like me) to an epic struggle with the cosmos (Bill Gates is reading my mind). Paranoid postures and thought systems are defensive phenomena that anticipate catastrophe, warding off disaster with ever more intricate narratives about enemies and their motives and fantasies of conspiracy and surveillance. They serve important purposes in our lives, emerging out of a fundamental need to identify vectors of harm, but can lock people into a debilitating anxiety and/or a state from which they inflict harm on people around them, whom they experience as threats and enemies. Paranoia, as Silvan Tomkins writes, is defined by a "strong theory of negative affect": fully activated, paranoia will mobilize a powerful interpretive apparatus behind its defense against hurt and humiliation. It can be so dedicated to the work of anticipating disaster, however, that it leaves no room for positive affect or feeling. The latter becomes "a luxury [the paranoid] cannot afford while he is engaged in warfare."[3]

Paranoia has strong formal properties. Paranoid thinking is mesmerizing, beautiful. It is patterned, mirrored, fractal, viral, spiraled, escalatory. Melanie Klein approached paranoia as a specific form of anxiety, a set of persecutory fears that yield a splitting of the world into bad and good objects. The term *schizoid* describes the splittings, cleavings, and fragmentations that proliferate in paranoid systems.[4] For Klein, the paranoid/schizoid position emerges quite early as a part of normative infant development. The child experiences the caretaker's body as part-objects that are furthermore split into objects of love and hate (e.g., "the good [gratifying] and bad [frustrating] breast"). In her model, psychosis grows out of crises in the working through of frustration, fear, and anger at this level, in which case the splitting necessary to the practice of living (recognizing that which is good, that which is bad; that which is nourishing, that which is toxic) develops into extremes of idealization and hatred and the adoption of binarized, warlike postures.[5] A frustrated desire may be projected and rewritten as a sense of persecution that demands destruction of the other (this person doesn't give me what I want; this person is bent on destroying me; I must destroy them before they destroy me). The paranoid subject might project the most loved and hated aspects of their own sense of self onto two people in their world, who then orbit each other (I must protect A from the machinations of B; A is honest and trustworthy, B a malicious fake). These are just a few expressions of the splitting, or schizoid, tendencies that define relatively everyday paranoid postures.

Sigmund Freud was arguably at his weakest when writing about paranoia. He had a very specific idea about what drove people to paranoid forms of delusion. Confronted with a person's persecutory delusion, Freud promises, "if we go into the matter only a little more deeply, we shall be able to see that the really operative factor in these social injuries lies in the part played in them by the homosexual components in affective life."[6] In his model, paranoid fixations always mask a homosexual problem. Projective dynamics express a prohibited, distorted, rerouted same-sex desire. He explains, "I, a man, love him (a man)," becomes "I (a man) am being persecuted by him (a man). I hate him."[7] This is, of course, homophobic. That said, "homosexual components" are written right onto the surface of my own case. Because of this, even knowing his theorizations are wrongheaded, when I tried to understand what had happened to and around me, I turned to an essay I'd read in school: Freud's "A Case of Paranoia Running Counter to the Theory of the Disease" (1915). Until I dug it out of my file cabinet, I'd forgotten that this case, like mine, centers on a woman with a workplace problem.

"Some years ago," Freud writes, "a well-known lawyer" sent a woman to him. A coworker had seduced her. She was afraid he was going to blackmail her with photographs that she feared he had secretly taken of their encounters. "By exhibiting these pictures," she worried, "he could bring shame upon her and force her to resign her position."[8] Although this essay has some importance in feminist psychoanalytic theory, I should say up front: in Freudian literature, this is a deep cut—it is not as developed as is his well-known (and also flawed) writing about Dora, for example. This essay, furthermore, is not a proper case history, as the woman in question did not seek treatment from him. When she showed up in her lawyer's office, she presented herself as a victim of a potential harassment campaign. The lawyer referred her to Freud so he might confirm a suspicion that his client was suffering from a paranoid delusion. Freud is interested in her delusion, which he takes as a given, because the orientation of her persecution complex appeared to challenge his theorization of paranoia as a defense against homosexual desire. Her sense of persecution seemed to grow around men, however, and was therefore not very queer at all.

We know her story only through Freud's telling of it. The man with whom she had this affair was a coworker; her anxiety took the form of a fear that because she had sex with a coworker she will lose her job. She was an employee at a "big institution" where she "held a responsible post" (98). She was the sole support for her aging mother. Although she was a "singularly attractive and handsome girl" (97), this thirty-year-old woman had had no serious romantic relationships. An "official" at the same institution where she worked, "a cultured and attractive man, had paid her attentions and she had inevitably been drawn towards him" (98). Freud notes that marriage was, "for external reasons" (98), out of the question.

She and her coworker had two clandestine meetings: "As he promised not to expose her to any risk, she had at last consented to visit him in his bachelor rooms in the daytime" (98). After one of the two trysts that she described, she saw two men in the hallway outside the man's rooms. They were carrying a box covered in cloth. During one of these meetings, she told Freud, she thought she heard a "kind of knock or tick" (98). It seemed to come from the direction of a window, which was partially obscured by a heavy curtain. Thinking of the cloth-covered box, she heard this noise as the click of a camera's shutter. She voiced her worry to her lover, who explained that what she heard was not the click of a camera, but the tick of a "small clock on a writing-desk" near the room's window. But no amount of persuasion on his part could dispel her anxiety. She became fixated on the idea that he had conspired to photograph her in flagrante.

Freud interprets her fixation on the noise of a camera's click as a projection of her own disordered desire. In his reading, she hears neither the tick of a clock nor the click of a camera. He argues instead, with a smug triumph ("I shall take the liberty of commenting" [98]), that the "knock" on which her story hinges is, in fact, the sonic projection of the throb of her clitoris: "I do not believe that the clock ever ticked or that any noise was heard at all. The woman's situation justified a situation of throbbing in the clitoris. This was what she subsequently projected as a perception of an external object" (105).

Our woman's case runs counter to Freud's theory of paranoia because the female patient is plagued by a paranoid fantasy that revolves around a male lover. Paranoia, in his view, operates as a defense against the "homosexual components of affective life." He subjects her story to a search for the woman for whom, theory predicted, the patient must have an unresolved same-sex attachment. This becomes her mother when it is revealed that her fear of losing her position takes the precise form of a fear that this male lover will show these photographs to her female boss—a white-haired older woman who, the patient tells Freud, reminds her of her mother (with whom, it should be noted, this patient lived: she was her mother's only child).

For Freud, the affinity between her mother and the "white-haired elderly manageress" (101) points to a particular sexual problem—the struggle of a daughter to mature and separate from her mother and allow herself to be a sexual subject in relation to men: "The woman's attachment to her own sex hinders her attempt to adopt a person of the other sex as a love-object. Love for the mother becomes the protagonist of all those tendencies which, act-ing as her 'conscience,' would arrest the girl's first step along the new road to normal sexual satisfaction, in many respects a dangerous one; and indeed, it succeeds in destroying her relationship with the man" (102). With the revelation of the secret of her lesbian attachments to older women, Freud closes the book on the problem she posed to his theory of paranoia.

This woman's fear/fantasy is compelling. As is the case for so many of Freud's texts, feminist readers tend to relate to the woman in this essay, and to her situation—not because Freud gets her, but because he seems so oblivious to what matters. The essay, Naomi Schor writes, "bears blatant witness to precisely that aspect of Freud's writing which has most angered his feminist critics: the unexamined priority and primacy of the male paradigm."[9] "A Case of Paranoia" has long served as a staging ground for scholars claiming paranoia for feminist theory. Jack Halberstam argues for the recovery of "the power of feminine paranoia, or simply feminist critique," from this woman's narrative.[10] Schor sees her fear/fantasy as "an exemplary instance of female theorizing," a theorizing that is, furthermore, "grounded in the body."[11] The cinematic character of her fixation on the possibility of having been subjected to photographic surveillance has made the essay interesting to feminist and lesbian feminist film criticism: it is important, for example, to Patricia White's influential writing on feminist theory and lesbian desire ("Female Spector, Lesbian Specter: *The Haunting*"). White unravels the disavowals of lesbian desire and lesbian possibility that limited not only Freud's work but feminist theory that leans on Freud's theorizations while disavowing homosexuality and homophobia as defining features of his writing about women and their desires for each other.

Where Freud saw paranoia as a displaced homosexual desire (a return of the repressed), queer theorists see paranoia's association with homosexuality as an effect of a homophobic culture. Thus, in and around queer theory, a lot of energy has collected around the subject.[12] "Paranoia," Eve Kosofsky Sedgwick explains, "is a uniquely privileged site for illuminating not homosexuality itself, as in the Freudian tradition, but rather precisely the mechanisms of homophobic and heterosexist enforcement against it."[13] Much of her book *Between Men* tracks the emergence of homophobia "not most immediately as an oppression of homosexual men, but as a tool for manipulating the entire spectrum of male bonds, and hence the gender system as a whole."[14]

Homosexual possibility haunts patriarchal, heterosexist institutions: the more intense the prohibitions of that institution, the more queerness it seems to produce. As Guy Hocquenghem writes, "the homosexuality which it represses and sublimates keeps springing from every pore of the social body."[15] One feels this in Freud's essay—we begin with a story in which there are no lesbians and end with a story in which lesbians seem to be everywhere—at home, at work, behind the curtain, and hidden in the walls.

As a student assigned "A Case of Paranoia" in feminist theory classes, I never questioned whether or not the woman in Freud's office was deluded: I had assumed that her fantasy spoke a patriarchal truth and that we could appreciate this without sleuthing the question of whether or not her accusation was reasonable. She might suffer from a delusion, but its nature speaks a truth about her experience. Today, however, I am struck by how familiar, by how normal her anxiety feels.

At the core of her anxiety is not only the idea that she was secretly photographed while having sex with her colleague, but that these photographs were being circulated at work and that her coworkers were bonding with each other over her humiliation. Examples of her worst-case scenario abound. The form of image-based abuse she feared—exploitation of her sexual vulnerability to shame her at work—is awfully close to what today is popularly known as revenge porn: the nonconsensual distribution of photographs, usually but not always produced within the context of a consensual sexual relationship.[16] Self-described revenge porn websites solicit detailed information about the people featured in uploaded files: names, social media accounts, hometowns, and, importantly, professions and employers.[17] This is a crowdsourced form of harassment keyed to drawing what feels private into the public: victims can be hounded, threatened, often at work, by consumers of these websites.[18] People subjected to this form of abuse can feel as if their world has been turned inside out and rendered uninhabitable: this is a severe and, indeed, paradigmatic invasion of privacy.

The scale and severity of this particular form of harassment is specific to contemporary digital media ecologies and the integration of photography into our erotic lives. Concern about violating uses of photography, however, dates back to the invention of small, portable cameras in the late nineteenth century. By the time Freud published his essay in 1915, the fact "that one might be photographed without one's knowledge or consent," Josh Lauer observes, "had become an uneasy fact of life."[19] "Detective cameras," as they were called, had been around for several decades, available in not only the form of the box that our woman believes she saw in the hands of a man in the hallway, but also disguised as books, pocket watches, and even clocks. The problem of surreptitious photography appears prominently in late nineteenth-century discourse about threats to personal privacy. A somewhat satirical 1884 *New York Times* article describes them as a "national scorn" that ruins vacations but also reputations. "Things have come to such a pass that no lady can step out of a carriage without the fear that every trip has been surreptitiously caught by a shameless camera, and no man can offer a lady the slightest attention and feel sure that his innocent action has not been forever perpetuated in gelatin emulsion as enduring as brass."[20] The photography bug, the author of this screed argues, makes people "wildly insane."

In their widely cited 1890 *Harvard Law Review* article, "The Right to Privacy," Louis D. Brandeis and Samuel D. Warren decry the "unauthorized circulation of portraits of private persons and the evil of invasion of privacy by the newspapers" as an attack on "sacred precincts of private and domestic life."[21] They called for a new legal shield that might protect the privacy of especially people like them, as Warren's wife Mabel was a socialite and a figure in the day's equivalent of gossip journalism.[22] "To satisfy a prurient taste," they write, "the details of sexual relations are spread broadcast in the columns of the daily papers. To occupy the indolent, column upon column is filled with idle gossip, which can only be procured by intrusion upon the domestic circle."[23] This reduces the reading public to their basest instincts, destroying "at once robustness of thought and delicacy of feeling. No enthusiasm can flourish, no generous impulse can survive under its blighting influence."[24] To underscore the urgency of this crisis, they draw from "The Photographic Nuisance," a letter to editors at the *Nation* (February 20, 1890) that describes portable, easy-to-hide cameras as "add[ing] a new horror to life." The author of that letter refers to the case of one woman who "has fortunately never known that her photograph was accidentally found adorning the rooms of a man recently arrested in Boston on a criminal charge, nor that her photograph was spoken of by him in such terms that would make the blood of any one having a spark of chivalry boil within him."[25] Her image travels from the man's wall to the police who arrested him to the men who prosecute the case to the men who report it for the papers and write editorials about the outrage. A growing circle of men bond over the image of this "young and lovely woman" whom they protect from understanding the nature of her own violation.

Patriarchal notions of privacy coddle and punish, promising security to those willing to be confined to its structures. Sexualized abuse and violence have an organizing force in our lives, not (only) because so many of us experience it, but because so many of the governing practices that touch our lives are built in its name. Each of these formations gives privileged (white, wealthy, cis) women access to a sense of privacy by nesting their entitlement in a paranoid defense against its ruination—an apprehensive fantasy about what might or could happen that naturalizes their dependency on white and patriarchal institutions. The fearful tremble of the wife justifies the hardening of the structure that contains her. Consider the conclusion of "Woman on the Farm," an infamous speech delivered by the Georgia politician Rebecca Felton to the Georgia Agricultural Society in 1897. Felton describes the myriad difficulties experienced by women in agriculture. She takes white men to task for their drunkenness, licentiousness, for their lack of economy, and for their refusal to recognize women's contributions to agriculture. In this speech's conclusion, their failure as men, as husbands and fathers, is not pinned to the abuse they heap on their own families but to a threat embodied by enfranchised Black men, whom Felton describes as "honey[ed] and snuggle[d]" for their vote. She conjures a racialized sense of sexual threat to generate mass concern for white women, whose situation is taken as an allegory for the state of the nation: "It is a disgrace in a free country," she declares, "when rape and violence are a public reproach and the best part of God's creation are trembling and afraid to be left alone in their homes. . . . If it requires lynching to protect woman's dearest possession from ravening human beasts, then I say lynch a thousand a week if it is necessary." This speech was reported by newspapers across the nation. When people spit the phrase "white feminism" with anger, they are citing the enabling of and complicity with these arrangements of race, sex, power, and violence, the forms of paranoia that define white and patriarchal spaces.[26]

That sense that an institution is supposed to look after you, protect you from the person making you feel afraid, anxious, ashamed—where does that come from? Who made that promise, really? The coddling/punishing expectations of normative feminine comportment around the private shaped Freud's response to the woman in his office. For him, her frank discussion of her sexual self is not evidence of her maturity, but of her madness: "Neither in her manner nor by any kind expression of emotion did she betray the slightest shame or shyness, although some such state of mind would naturally arise on such an occasion in the presence of a stranger" (98). She is frank, unashamed, and yet also petrified by the idea that an image of her sexual self might become public.

Toxic expressions of a right to privacy do not negate the fact that an access to a sense of the private is essential to a sense of self: it is the space from which a sense of the personal emerges. This is why it is such deeply contested political terrain. As Jennifer Nash writes, "The private can function as a radical site for culturally marginalized subjects who may envision the private as a critical site of safety."[27] Edouard Glissant argues for the importance of opacity and the need to not be transparent to, graspable by the other.[28] In a digital context, "privacy," writes Josh Lauer, "might usefully be described as the ability to suspend the emission of evidence about oneself—the right to be non-communicative."[29]

While I was in the middle of processing the fact that my stalker had been surveilling and recording me, news broke of an awful case at Rutgers University. A student, Tyler Clementi, died from suicide after he learned that his roommate had used a computer in their room to stream one of his hookups, so he could watch it with friends. Just a few days passed between Clementi's discovery of this invasion of his privacy and his death. When I learned about the case, I understood how a young person could be made so desperate by this violation. I wrote about the case in *Campus Sex, Campus Security*:

> For people not used to living under explicit surveillance, finding oneself stripped of a sense of privacy is profoundly disturbing. The experience of exposure doubles on itself. One comes to grips with how much work a sense of privacy does to maintain a specific kind of self-hood—and also with how much that work had depended on a fiction. It is a shift, a heightening of one's understanding. That sense of privacy gives us our shape—our psychic skin. The sense of an inside and an outside—it is a foundational fiction. Even a movement in that boundary (me/not me) can be traumatic— but its sudden evaporation? (55–56)

Those sentences draw from my experience of learning that I was being recorded secretly, of not knowing where that surveillance began or ended, in order to make sense of the intensity of Clementi's crisis. The sense of privacy is not just a matter of law. It is a deeply social experience that gives shape to the sense of self and others. When I describe the sense of privacy as depending on a fiction, I mean the following: every day we disavow our awareness of the fact that we are the subject of a wide array of surveillance practices, or could be. People living inside jails, prisons, and hospitals do not have the luxury of being unaware of the eyes on them, nor do families under the surveillance of welfare systems, children in the foster care system, immigrants and the undocumented, people seeking abortions and gender-affirming care in places where these are criminalized, and people under treatment for sexually transmitted and stigmatized disease. I could go on. The dismantling of privacy that goes with each of these positions troubles the soul in its own way.

When I described the sense of privacy as a kind of psychic skin, I was experimenting with the language of the psychoanalyst Didier Anzieu, whose practice centers the relationship between psychic and corporeal integrity. Anzieu argued for the "skin ego" as an essential component of the experience of self and identity, serving as a "psychical wrapping."[30] Developed in and through touch, this experience produces a sense of the body's limits, its ending and its beginning. The skin ego is one type of "psychic" or "psychical" envelope, meaning a material and sensorial container for alignment of being and self. His work addresses the vital importance of things like sound, smell, sight, and taste to our psychic shape and its integrity: his language is particularly compelling for understanding how deeply our bodies hold, incorporate, express, and are shaped by crises in that sense of shape.[31] The formation of these psychic envelopes is not a given: it is a development, and it is essential to the formation of self-awareness. This branch of psychoanalysis considers not the content of our fears and fantasies so much as the way the self is experienced as shapes and forms.

Anzieu worked with what he called the "formal signifier," by which he means "a signifier of configuration" of our sense of shape, our experience of an environment, and the dynamism of our relationship to others and the world.[32] The formal signifier registers fear and anxiety as a crisis in form. "These signifiers," he writes, "are psychic representations not only of certain instincts, but also of various forms of organization of the self and the ego. . . . In this sense, formal signifiers are primarily representations of psychic containers." One patient, for example, sought out Anzieu because she felt "her skin was shrinking, this was driving her mad, and she was afraid of losing her identity."[33] She described herself as "a skin of troubles."[34] In Anzieu's terms, the woman in Freud's office felt herself becoming an image that she could not see. A crisis in a sense of privacy is a crisis of this order. For R. D. Laing, the development of the sense of a "territory of ourselves" in which "there can be only our footprints" is "the basis of genuine relationship." In a schizoid state, a person "feels both more exposed, more vulnerable to others than we do, and more isolated. Thus a schizophrenic may say that he is made of glass, of such transparency and fragility that a look directly at him splinters him into bits and penetrates straight through him."[35]

Behind ruminations like this is the haunting sense of dread I felt when the people administering the case at school told me that N had been recording me, but that they could not tell me where, when, or how.

Freud's analysis steps over the problem written across the surface of this woman's story and built into the architecture of her paranoid fantasy: it is a workplace complaint.

As I spent time with Freud's essay, I found more and more harmonies with my own situation.

In the beginning, N's story was simple: my role as a teacher prohibited me from expressing my true feelings. Then, as the school prohibited her from contacting me, actually existing institutional structures seemed to affirm that narrative. This also seemed to intensify her sense of persecution—the forces that required the encoding of our relationship grew in scale, and my own place in the story mutated. At the student conduct hearing, she described me as "engag[ing] in over-the-top conversations regarding sex and related subjects."[36] She described us as in a relationship, the evidence for which was my work. She accused me of retaliating against her by engineering my own stalking—writing the emails, sending the flowers, posting comments on my blog, and so on. It was, she claimed, all me. She presented me as a repressed lesbian who was jealous of N and her partner, because they had a baby. She told the Student Conduct Committee that would eventually clear her that I had become vindictive after she "critiqued" an essay I published on abortion. She used the fact that I'd had an abortion (mentioned in that essay) to shore up this story about my jealousy. She told colleagues that, shortly after the birth of their child, I'd reported N to social services: I was, in this story, intent on destroying her family because she had what I wanted. I did not do these things. But there is a reason why my writing on abortion featured in her defense against the accusation that I was harassing her.

I think of a specific time in my life as the primary context for her stalking behavior: the two-year period when I met S, fell in love, and grieved our relationship, and when Eve died. When S and I met, I was writing about abortion. Early in our relationship, when he asked me about my work, we talked about this. We shared our own feelings about reproduction and sexuality. Early in our relationship I told him an anecdote about sitting at a table with a bunch of friends who were talking about wanting to have children. I interrupted the evening's amiable flow with the story of the abortion I had during my first semester at college. I made the experience into a picaresque, happy adventure. My anecdote was honest, but deliberately oppositional, and even aggressive. When we talked about that evening and my bad behavior (I was embarrassed that I couldn't just keep quiet and let people enjoy a sense of their future), S said he wished he had access to a rhetorical intervention like that, which might allow him to neatly describe, performatively enact, his own relationship to these forms of compulsory, reproductive heterosexuality.

I'd never heard a straight guy say that. It was an unguarded statement about his experience of gender and difference. It moved me, and it helped me to understand the discourse of abortion in an expanded sense—it helped me to appreciate the specific position of the reproductive body as always already a figure for abortion. The body ascribed with the potential to become pregnant is loaded with abortive possibility, with the power to refuse possibility—and this, for him, was enviable. He liked, even coveted, this kind of refusal. I got the sense that he found this sexy. I could see that in the conversation that I'd described to him, I was aborting—I spun the tale out, made it funny, gross, weird—I'd thrown myself out of the circle with a light-hearted story about this thing that's supposed to be not only unfunny, but traumatic. Even now, so many years later, when I think about talking with S, I feel the pleasure of those conversations, and I miss him. In those moments, we really felt each other. (Right now, on this page, I am being the scholar N described: atypical as an academic, and, from certain perspectives, even extremely so. I am being "over the top," in conversation about "sex and related subjects.") I published my essay on abortion and queer theory in the journal *Qui Parle*.[37] This was the essay that N mentioned in the hearing.

When I first turned to the campus for help, the staff handling harassment complaints told me that I needed to prove that the anonymous emails and unwanted gifts (directed at my personal email account and sent to my home address) were related to my job: otherwise, this harassment was not the school's problem.

I learned about a service that works like certified mail, identifying the IP address and general location (e.g., city, county, state) for the computer used by anyone who reads email messages sent through its platform. Around this time, N had emailed me from her school account to ask me to send her a copy of my essay. I sent the article back to her, as a reply. I then sent a message replying to one of the anonymous emails. I sent both through this platform and shared what I learned with the campus: given their IP addresses, the emails were likely from the same person and were sent from Southern California. I gave our Title IX investigator copies of those reports.

When she was interviewed as a part of the Title IX investigation, the campus shared this material with N: she was told that I'd used this program to establish a link between N and the anonymous accounts. I used my writing on abortion as a lure, and N knew it. Looking back, knowing what I know now, I wish I had not shared that report with the school.

It felt as if, within the institution's structure and systems, N and I were two sides of a coin. The campus's complaint system threw me into a gothic space in which N's pathology was cast across the entire institution. It startled me: her crisis seemed to harmonize with the university's processes and systems—one thing seemed to amplify the other. They patterned my life. She couldn't see the difference between us: the world radiated her desires back to her as if they were mine. And the school couldn't see the difference between us either. Her behavior, my own responses to it, and the administrative processes managing the crisis that grew around me were so in tune with each other that it felt like, at work, my job was to stay in that space of insecurity and fear. It felt as if, in my work environment, my job was to absorb, to *live* harassment.

This crisis seemed to draw out a madness in the institution itself. At a particularly desperate moment, I came across an article on "risk management in the stalking situation." Its six authors approach stalking as a "social problem, often driven by psychiatric disorder in its perpetrators and productive of psychological and social damage in its victims."[38] Addressing readers likely to find themselves managing stalking/harassment dynamics in and through an institutional context (campus investigators and case managers, for example), they insist that stalking cases not be framed as a conflict, in which parties are understood as having opposed interests: doing so enlists the institution in the stalking dynamic. They explain:

> There is a conflict between the stalker's desires and the victim's interests, but they are at one in being at risk of damage from the stalking situation. There can be a tragic symmetry between the victim forced to live an increasingly restricted life in a state of constant fear and the stalker's devoting all his or her time and resources to a futile and ultimately frustrating pursuit. Both the victim's and the perpetrator's lives can be laid waste. This is not to argue for equivalence between victim and perpetrator. In stalking, there are real victims and real perpetrators; one offends and the other is offended against. However, they share the chance of disaster. These perspectives, which encompass the risks to stalkers and victims, have

the advantage for health professionals of minimizing the ethical dilemma concerning whose interests one is serving: the patient's or the victim's.[39]

The difficulty of the stalking situation grows from the entanglement of the living situations for aggressor and victim. The relationship is an intensely nonconsensual form of social relation. I went through long stretches of time in which my movements in the world were limited by fear. I could not walk from my car to my office without anxiety. I dreaded all forms of visibility. I knew enough about my stalker to feel pretty sure of the following, however: as much as my own life felt increasingly constricted by her harassment of me, she was suffering too, if differently.

I did not feel like my skin was shrinking. I felt like something was hovering over me, something frightening that others saw and that I could sense only by tracking their reactions to me. I felt haunted. Burdensome.

Over time, the things that gave me pleasure drifted away. The darkness that was hovering over me settled onto and into me. As it absorbed me, I lost my form.

I returned to Freud's essay, and to writing on paranoia more generally, because I was trying to understand what I was going through, not only as the object of another person's delusion, but as someone who was being driven to paranoia by workplace betrayals that pivoted on a story about me, as a sexual person and as a figure not just within the institution, but for and of it. I was struggling with the fact that so much of what happened was between women—me, N, the students who helped her, and the women who administered the case. It mattered to me that we handled things so badly. I felt betrayed, let down, humiliated, angry, useless.

Over the years, I turned to colleagues looking for help or even just some understanding, but I could feel their unease at the baggy weirdness of my story. When I talk about these things at work, I'm not my best self. When I look at the archive of my emails to the student conduct staff, to various deans, my department chair, chief campus counsel, I am horrified by who I became as I moved through the procedural gauntlet. My emails grew more and more unwieldy: I explained, demonstrated, argued, begged, and lamented. My literary output reached its zenith in a very, very long email written after the hearing that outlined what had happened and how it was impacting me. I pointed to those aspects of Title IX and antidiscrimination law that addressed what I was going through, and offered brief summaries of best practices for managing workplace harassment. I tried to explain why that hearing was so damaging. I tried to make useful observations. I can laugh at these things now. What did I think these tracts would accomplish? What did I imagine any of these people would do? I can't believe anyone actually read those emails, and I don't blame them.

I was filing complaints, carrying grievances, and struggling to hold onto the parts of my life that were not defined by harassment. I was sitting in offices talking to people who thought I was crazy. And I felt crazy. It was not sustainable. Even now, so many years later, even with some distance on the crisis, I am startled by how quickly anger wells up in me, especially at work. And so I have tried to find a way back to myself. I figured if I couldn't wriggle out from underneath paranoia's spiraling knowledge problems, I might as well fold my arms around them.

Sara Ahmed has described the complaint as "a phenomenology of the institution."[40] A case of harassment is a story about the relationship between the detail, the individual, and the structure in and through which harassment is staged. It requires theorization. You find yourself wrestling with the relationship between the system and the things that are happening to you, which feel personal and cling to your body. Patriarchy, capitalism, neoliberalism, white supremacy, the administration—these figures march across your case, rendering the exceptional thing you are enduring into something symptomatic, inevitable. To learn to live with a case is to learn how to ride out paranoia's highs (it's all related!) and lows (I'm doomed!).

When our woman first appears in Freud's office, it is not as a woman struggling with her repressed homosexuality but, as Naomi Schor observes in her essay on the case, as a member of "that class of paranoiacs known as *quérulants*."[41] The choice of language here is Schor's. The *quérulante*, or querulous, is a specific kind of paranoid. We first meet her at the intersection of law and psychiatry, in the middle of the nineteenth century. German criminologist Johan Ludwig Casper dedicates several pages to *Querulantenwahn* in his 1857 handbook on forensic medicine. Those suffering from "the litigant's delusion" are, he writes, "individuals who, when what they consider as rights belonging to them have been denied them by consistent and repeated judicial decisions, have their minds thus deeply and permanently shaken and more and more depressed. In their desire, becoming ever more impetuous, to attain and achieve their fancied rights, they dissipate their means, they importune the courts of justice, from the lowest to the highest, with continually fresh memorials and complaints, they study the common law, day and night, and ruin their bodily and mental health ever more and more."[42] This person's sense of grievance intensifies and shifts, it scales up, ensnaring more and more people, absorbing more and more resources. Psychiatrists of the period debated the nature of the querulous alongside that of the homosexual and the hysteric. Is delusional querulousness a psychological disorder triggered by a grievance, they wanted to know, or was it more physical? Was it treatable? Discourses of the law, psychiatry, and sexology mingle in the querulous for whom, Richard von Krafft-Ebing writes, "there is a formal pleasure in lawsuits."[43] What does it mean that this pathology is so specific, so organic to justice systems?[44]

The vexatious, paranoid, and "unusually persistent" complainant is a problem for employers and for court systems, and the subject of scholarship advising those who administer their grievances. Paul Mullen and Grant Lester, in their work addressing this professional space, offer a typology of complainants as well as management strategies keyed to addressing the challenges of the most difficult.[45] Normal complainants, they reassure managers, engage the process to seek "legitimate redress." They have a healthy sense of scale: their grievance does not take over their life. Their complaint is focused and specific, and they are open to an achievable settlement. A difficult or unreasonable complainant is "emotional and easily angered." They see themselves as victimized. They are, in this typology, "entitled and overoptimistic [in their] expectations of compensation." They are "difficult to negotiate with" and are reluctant to accept other perspectives on their situation. They can be "persistent, demanding and occasionally threatening" but "will ultimately settle" even if they feel that settlement isn't fair. Like the normal complainant, they will relinquish their grievance rather than allow it to consume them.

For querulous paranoids and vexatious litigants, however, there is a strong risk that their lives will become so entangled in the complaint process that they are consumed, even destroyed by it. The woman in Freud's office is there because her lawyer is afraid she belongs to this category. For these complainants, there is no achievable resolution: their narratives may involve not just compensation, but an escalating need for personal vindication and retribution. These kinds of complainants might be responding to an accusation against them, lashing back at an accusation with their own complaints and lawsuits. Or they might enter into a complaint process in response to a specific injury, which might be real, imagined, or an imaginative take on a something real but minor. Their grievances accumulate, and the scale of the struggle grows. This complainant can lose track of reality. Within this group, one finds thought distortions and patterns of escalation that can become malignant. "Querulousness" in a complainant "involves not just persistence but a totally disproportionate investment of time and resources in grievances that grow steadily from the mundane to the grandiose, and whose settlement requires not just apology, reparation, and/or compensation but retribution and personal vindication."[46] A complaint about the miscalculation of a savings account balance develops into a complaint against the World Bank, for example. These complainants become identified with this form of struggle. Through it all, this complainant fights for their day in court with a conviction that this will bring them an epic form of validation. (In their research, this group of scholars have found that a minority of unusually persistent complainants suffer from schizophrenia—in such cases, complaints may be incoherent and/or bizarre.) These scholars work as consultants and teach administrators to understand that these escalations are not inevitable, and that a person with querulous tendencies is not destined to become an administrative nightmare, if their complaints are handled in a manner that acknowledges their grievance without overservicing it, and if managers, for example, invite the complainant to participate in de-escalation.

These typologies are fun to think with, but they have their limits. Mullen and Lester discuss a set of complainants who can be quite difficult, but for good reason: social reformers. "Social reformers are pursuing issues of concern to groups of their fellow citizens," they explain, "and they use personal experience, if they use it at all, to inform their campaigns."[47] These complainants are challenging for administrators because they engage in a complaint process not only out of a sense of personal grievance but in the hope of effecting some form of systemic change—or, at least, out of a desire to prevent what happened to them from happening to others. They ask a lot of their institutions and may be difficult to appease. Reading through this literature, one learns that it is not easy for administrators to distinguish one kind of complainant from the other. A wide variety of complainants make connections between their grievances and big-picture thinking. Unusually persistent, vexatious/querulous, and schizophrenic complainants will frame their complaint in terms of justice—a complainant's assertion that their grievance is meant to address a systemic form of injustice may, in fact, be received by case managers as a red flag. Making things even more difficult: social reformer complainants may also be whistleblowers, meaning their complaint exposes a systemic form of corruption in which the very people supervising them and administering complaints are implicated. These people are vulnerable to severe gaslighting from the accountable organization.[48] "Whistle blowers, who usually claim to be exposing nefarious and corrupt practices in their place of work," Mullen and Lester explain, "are a particularly difficult group in which to separate altruistic from querulous behavior."[49] Because a whistleblower's employer is usually working actively to suppress the information they are exposing, it can be hard for people handling complaints to see the difference between the whistleblower and the vexatious/querulous complainant—whistleblower complaints are, by definition, startling in terms of the scale of the scandal they are naming. Their "accusations often turn on an interpretation of events that may seem questionable, or even implausible, to those without their inside knowledge."[50] They may be characterized as querulous or vexatious complainants, in fact, in order that their complaint might be suppressed. An institution may be so rooted in the practices of disavowal that enable the corruption at issue that it experiences complaints about it as an existential threat.

Which am I? Am I difficult? A social reformer? Querulous? Was I too grand in my complaint? Too modest?

Within a patriarchal society it is hard to not see sexual harassment and sexual assault as part of a systemic problem. Complaints of sexual harassment and assault challenge the social fabric of the institutions in which they occur, whether that be within a family or a university. For people with these kinds of complaints, justice is rarely achieved, in part because what looks and feels like justice requires systemic change, and the offices that manage sexual harassment complaints are usually walled off from the institutional processes that actually do make a difference.[51] Our sense of justice is often not reasonable, by administrative standards. We are difficult. When we persist, we are vexatious. And when we argue the links between what happened to us and, say, what has happened or may happen to others, we may become querulous.

HOME AT WORK, WORK AT HOME

Freud considered paranoid delusions to be untreatable. In a 1911 essay on Daniel Schreber's memoir of his mental illness, he writes, "We cannot accept patients [like him], or at least retain them for very long, given that we set the prospect of therapeutic success as a precondition for our treatment."[52] His observations on paranoid psychoses are thus developed at arm's length, staged in the domain of theory and interpretation rather than that of a healing practice. This attitude limits his approach to the woman sitting in his office. He does not believe she can be helped by either a lawyer or a doctor. And she is there not because she wants his help; she is there because she poses a managerial problem for her lawyer.

Freud seems oblivious to the risks associated with having a sexual relationship with a coworker. He shows no curiosity at all about that dimension of this woman's complaint (not surprising given how very recently common sense on this has shifted). This woman's complaint describes the translation of a consensual form of intimacy into a nonconsensual form of publicity, in which her sexual body is revealed within the social context of the workplace. The idea of this exposure feels, to her, like annihilation. The idea of this photograph has a material force in her life: it is the very manifestation of her vulnerability. She heard the sound of an opening and enclosure. A click, a flicker. The private is public. An escape is captured. Time is stolen from work (their daytime meetings); it is then accounted for (as snapshots of these stolen moments return to the workplace to haunt and punish her). The men around her experience this "click" differently: the capture of time stolen from work (the "tick of the clock on the desk"), the "throb" of the inside pushing out (the beating of the heart, the pulse of desire). But for her, that sound represents a kind of puncture and a fixing, a trap and a form of destruction ("my sexual self is stolen and distributed," "my sexual self has ruined my work").

The workplace, which is so very prominent as the scene of crisis in her story, is all but completely absent from Freud's analysis and from nearly all critical engagement with this text. It is treated as mere background. Sexual intimacy with a coworker is, for the woman in Freud's story, associated with a visual reproduction of the scene of their encounter and the illicit distribution of that image within the workplace. This photograph, she imagines, documents their daytime meetings; it captures the two of them as they steal time from the working day.

In her fear/fantasy, she is punished for traversing the divisions that organize her world, separating her home from her work. Those divisions are particularly challenging for women. Karl Marx observes that the worker "is at home when he is not working and when he is working he is not home."[53] He is "outside himself" when he works.[54] Once productive labor has been externalized and abstracted (e.g., clocking in to work on a factory's assembly line), what remains in the wake of that extraction is an assemblage of need. There is the part of you that is good for work, and there is the part of you left after you've put in your hours—the part of you that needs to eat, sleep, fuck, and play. Gendered dynamics within patriarchal and capitalist systems leave women meeting the reproductive needs of the worker; her meaning and value as a woman are expressed in the domain of those things that are marked as beyond price—sex, romance, love, and care. To accept money for these forms of labor is to sink into the space of the stigmatized. If the system benefits the capitalists to whom the worker's labor belongs, it is because behind the paid worker is the unpaid, unacknowledged labor of wives and mothers providing the reproductive labor for the family. These women are shadowed by an army of underpaid service and sex workers laboring in the criminalized margins—the latter's social abjection signals what one risks when one moves one's work into sex, and sex into one's work.

The camera miniaturizes the scenario of their encounter: that cloth-covered box describes sex's enclosure and sex as a form of enclosure. "No matter how many screams, sighs, and erotic exercises we make in bed," Silvia Federici writes, "we know that is a parenthesis and tomorrow both of us will be back in our civilized clothes (we will have coffee together as we get ready for work)."[55] That parenthesis holds the sense of one's life apart from one's work and keeps work out of one's life. That, at least, is the mythology. Our lives are not carved up this neatly: you can't tease these things apart from each other. The truth is that the workplace is a sexual space, and people who work together create and inhabit forms of sexual community. This grounding conflict subordinates the living labor of the bedroom and the kitchen to Work (productive/paid labor), folding reproductive labor into systems of enclosure, ensuring that "every moment of our lives functions for the accumulation of capital," even—or especially—those moments that feel like an escape.[56] The binaries that cluster around work (work/life; public/private; production/consumption) are not divisions so much as they are contradictions sustained by powerful forms of disavowal.[57] That is a kind of skin: a protective shield, which allows us to function as if these divisions were organic, stable, reliable givens and actually good for us.

Sexism is baked into commonsense logics regarding workplace harassment. What constitutes harassment is informed by how sex and work are defined—by what counts as sex, and by what does not count as work, and where and when work happens.[58] The organizations holding much of our lives, Joan Acker observes, are "gendered processes in which both gender and sexuality have been obscured through a gender-neutral, asexual discourse." An antiharassment practice requires a confrontation with the fact that "gender, the body, and sexuality are part of the process of control in work organizations."[59] Feminists who study organizational and institutional life address sex, gender, and sexuality as core components of these structures. Even the "the concept of 'a job,'" Acker writes, "is an implicitly gendered concept" insofar as a job is imagined as an empty space filled by a disembodied worker.[60] The ideal worker has no concerns that press against or limit their ability to fulfill that job's responsibilities. None of us are ideal workers. To be good at our jobs, many of us have to cultivate a sense of distance between work and life. When things are going well, one space can feel like a relief from the burdens of the other. Often, however, things do not go well. Work drags us out of our lives; our lives drag us out of our work. When you are going through it, you feel a deep sense of shame about the way it infects your whole life.

Workplace harassment and discrimination depend upon the disavowal of these enclosures and the painful conflicts they inflict on us. Sexual harassment's particularity is anchored in the exploitation of the disavowals that cling to sex as a thing that happens only in the bedroom, as a side of yourself fraught with potential for humiliation. Confrontations with harassment yield a crisis for the workplace because they surface the "schizophrenic character of sexual relations": the self is scattered, and we are plagued by the anxiety of tracking its bits and pieces.[61]

Queer paranoid figures haunt the workplace because it is patriarchy's paradigmatic social space. "Masculine structures and behaviors are conflated with work," writes Ann McGinley in her analysis of sexual harassment and the operations of workplace masculinities. The performance of certain kinds of masculinity (by men, for men) is "conflated with work and management techniques" and staged almost uniformly against bodies associated with feminine and reproductive labor.[62] Paranoia's privileged relationship with homosexuality has everything to do with the disavowal of the same-sex erotics that haunt patriarchal, homosocial, and hierarchical social structures (e.g., sports teams, the military, many churches, government). These kinds of structures are in and of themselves paranoid instruments. In her writing on the relationship between the prohibition of homosexual desire and the forms of attachment that organize the homosocial, Sedgwick asks us to consider "the operations necessary to deploy male-male desire as the glue rather than as the solvent of a hierarchical male disciplinary order."[63] In posing this question, Sedgwick wants us to contemplate the work that goes into making sex into a form of subjection and exploitation, rather than, say, a form of generosity. She wants us to consider the role of desire and its disavowal in the distribution of power. The sexualized abuse staged within hazing rituals, the sexual harassment of subordinates, the stigmatization of trans lives, the erasure of gay and lesbian history—these social practices reproduce biased forms of knowledge production and abusive structures of power. What manifestations of sex, what forms of sexual expression, what representations of sexual life reinforce hierarchical and abusive power structures? What manifestations of sex threaten them? What does it mean to confront the sexual practices that lie beneath the surface of an institution? Can the sexual culture of a workplace be transformed? In that last question I show some of my cards: you change the sexual culture of a workplace by changing the structure of the workplace. The former requires the latter.

This is the problem haunting the woman in Freud's office. We are encouraged in our fear of the collapse of our private and our public lives; we nurture panic regarding the consequences of these forms of exposure. This form of paranoia is normalized, socially prescribed. It is the hallmark of a respectable employee. What could be worse, we gasp, than the circulation of the image of your sexual self? Freud's reading, which collapses the camera, the clock, and the *quérulante*'s clit, performs this entangling of reproduction and the working day without enlightening us as to how and why her desire should take this spooky form. Freud makes a similar move elsewhere in writing on a teenage girl's obsessive nighttime rituals:

> Our patient gradually came to learn that it was as symbols of the female genitals that clocks were banished from her equipment for the night. Clocks and watches—though elsewhere we have found other symbolic interpretations for them—have arrived at a genital role owing to their relation to periodic processes and equal intervals of time. A woman may boast that her menstruation behaves with the regularity of clockwork. Our patient's anxiety, however, was directed in particular against being disturbed in her sleep by the ticking of a clock. The ticking of a clock may be compared with the knocking or throbbing in the clitoris during sexual excitement.[64]

As he does with our anxious coworker, Freud produces the girl's body as a kind of sex machine. A dread of the following day, the climbing of anxiety with each tick—of course ticking clocks drive an insomniac mad. Who does not know the grip of that late-night despair; who has not felt anxiety's proximity to desire? Of course, the grinding regularity of that tick might telescope out to the time of life itself. But while the clit might be said to "throb" with the beat of one's heart, it can't exactly be said to pulse according to a lunar cycle.

That said, the move from clit to cosmos is just the kind of rapid escalation that makes paranoid delusions exhilarating.

In her article on "A Case of Paranoia" and its *quérulant*, Schor treats Freud's focus on the complainant's clit as an opportunity to address the material of the sexual body; she repurposes his problematic turn for feminist theory. Provisionally accepting the mapping of the paradigm of the female hysteric onto the vaginal (in order to mobilize that paradigm against itself), Schor posits the clitoris as the anchor for a female—here meaning feminist—form of paranoia, which she imagines as an insistently materialist practice of theory making oriented by "the detail figure," or the synecdoche.[65] "The clitoris," she observes, "is coextensive with the detail."[66] It is coextensive with a kind of detail that "juts out" above the "planar surface of the text."[67] This synecdochic detail stands for the body to which it is attached but seems to also signal its potential escape (as in the "hand" one lends to another). We might build on Schor's attention to the slippery detail and respond to her call for a radically different way of listening to each other as we struggle with the acknowledgment of what we already know but disavow. In a sense, the *quérulante*'s clit is most definitely the issue. That clit emerges not from her discourse, but from Freud's. It is his sense of her problem that is the problem.

Within the space of collective disavowal, the sexual body of the sexed worker is an assemblage of provocative details threaded into paranoid networks— networks defined by the masculinist, homosocial dynamics Sedgwick described. Colleagues joke anxiously about whether they can hug one another and go home to former students who have become their wives. Women sit in boardrooms and stare out the window as men laugh at each other's jokes. Pundits lament the death of sex itself and imagine the university campus as taken over by an army of junior *quérulants*. Who is the rightful paranoid in such a world?

The woman in Freud's office slept with a coworker and is anxious she might lose her job because of it. This aspect of her fear is reasonable: it is a healthy kind of paranoia. Her anxiety is pathological only insofar as it has (maybe) settled into the form of a specific delusion rather than, say, a diffused sense of vulnerability—the latter being the hallmark of proper feminine comportment. It is, again, a socially acceptable form of paranoia ("all men are out to corrupt you"). Her problem originates in the accumulation of the differences represented by her lover, her mother, and her boss: paranoia emerges as a defense against an oppressive anxiety regarding the integrity of the social bonds organizing her work life, which, furthermore, sustain the relationship of her life to her work. These forces pressure her to become a woman like her mother—even as their survival depends on just the opposite. Unless, that is, she is supported by a man who will support them both—and, for reasons never specified by Freud, her lover-colleague is not that.

The complainant sent to Freud's office at the request of her lawyer is caught in the sexual and social contradictions that ground her workplace. Within the social structures organizing capital, sex is not only administered as that which happens outside the sphere of work; it is positioned as the opposite of work. One space appears as the projection of the other. The sexed subject straddles the division between productive and reproductive labor in a value system built on the rendition of the reproductive as beyond or underneath that system. Leopoldina Fortunati writes, "Within reproduction the elements concerned, the family, prostitution, labor power, the exchanges, and their relations of production are not actually recognized as being agents of elements of capitalist production. Here the process of mystification occurred a long way back, so far back indeed that the content of the relations of production within reproduction do not seem to have ever represented an exchange between women and capital, but between her and her male worker."[68] That mystification supports the "primitive accumulation" of reproductive labor. A wife is no ball and chain. She is, instead, capital's loamy ground. The drive is, always, to mine every fungible element from the domain of life making, and when you think you've run out, you punch through to another layer of profit. This is a grim view of the relationship between sex and work. We must insist on this line of thinking, however; we must remember the difficulty of the relationship of sex and work to each other if we want to understand why harassment is so endemic in institutional life, and why sexual harassment complaints, in particular, tend to have little impact on the context in which that harassment was staged. Each new complaint generates a scandal, a collective gasp from within the impacted professional community, and a round of moral panic. And yet nothing seems to change.

Sex is at once the site of mystification and material extraction—it is the scene of a crime, the nature of which is rendered into a timeless mystery in order that this crime might live on as its own machine of perpetual motion. From a Marxist-feminist angle, the argument against sexual harassment is not only anchored in a moral prohibition against the use of power and authority to coerce sex from subordinates. One also opposes sexual harassment because it absorbs sexed and raced subjects into a work economy predicated on the splitting off and minimization of the value of their reproductive labor, whether that worker is raped or married. That nauseating syntactical turn—"raped or married"—is, on my part, a deliberate rhetorical turn against the discourse that represents sexual coercion as the exception rather than our system's rule. What does it mean to be present to that fact?

The argument against harassment must not hinge on the patrolling of the boundary between sex and work, nor can it settle on the ritual of trial and expulsion as our collective problem's solution. Harassment is an effect of that division of labor: sex shadows and haunts the antisexual workplace. This fact shapes the jury that writes the verdict and the committee that hears the complaint. The resistance to harassment is, potentially, in this sense, a form of antiwork—the resistance to harassment can unravel the very idea of what work is. But to do that, such forms of resistance must insist on surfacing the sexual dimension of labor and all forms of labor relations. To do so is to attempt to wrestle the antiharassment struggle from the managerial structures that, in the name of protecting workers, make the workplace more sexist rather than less, not because Title IX enforcement (for example) makes sex on campus impossible or because the university is more likely to demote and fire feminists and queers in the name of sexual safety, but because these organizational structures naturalize and reinforce a sexed division of labor and furthermore produce sex as a form of entitlement, as a property to which one has rights, as a quality that lives only in the sense of the private, rather than an aspect of our common—meaning communal, meaning collective—life. These managerial practices (e.g., blanket bans against all sexual relationships between people within an organization, or between people of different positions in that organization's hierarchy) deepen the vulnerability of sexual subjects. Not only do such policies force sexual relationships underground (making the confrontation with abuse even harder), they reinforce the collective disavowal of the fact that work is always already sexed.

And so we might read this case of paranoia, that of the *quérulante*, as the story of a woman who hears what her colleagues disavow. If, on her return to the office, she sees in conversations between her lover and her boss signs of a sexual conspiracy, perhaps she is not wrong. And if Freud sees her as having a problem with her mother and her boss, perhaps he is not wrong either, insofar as her mother is the *quérulante*'s housewife, and as such, she haunts the woman who works and in whose wages her labor is hidden.

When she accepted her male coworker's invitation to an affair, the *quérulante* shed the skin of disavowal that had enabled her movement between home and the world. What, on finding herself naked in the office, was this "handsome girl" with a remarkable lack of shame to do?

4

HARASSMENT AND THE PRIVILEGES OF UNKNOWING

The Case of Larry Nassar

I n the United States, contemporary discourse about campus-based sexual harassment clusters around Title IX, an amendment to the Higher Education Act that regulates federal funding for schools.[1] Title IX requires that schools address the problem of sex-based forms of discrimination, and it structures the processes used by campus administrators to address discrimination, harassment, and abuse involving students. It promises that "no person in the United States shall, on the basis of sex, be excluded from participation in, be denied the benefits of, or be subjected to discrimination under any education program or activity receiving Federal financial assistance." The question of what "the basis of sex" means and what, about sex, is knowable drives the evolution, expansion, and contraction of Title IX's reach. Uncertainty about what "the basis of sex" means shapes the experience of harassment and discrimination, and it impacts every aspect in the administration of a case. Because my own case was shaped by my campus's poor understanding of this question and the requirements of this legislation, I became curious about not only this law but also how discourse about it factors into discourse about harassment on college campuses.

When Title IX passed into law in 1972, people had little sense of where it would lead us. It has been central to the rapid development of women's sports in the United States but also to the normalization of sex segregation in sports. It has facilitated the recognition of sexual assault and sexual harassment as aspects of sex discrimination in education—one of the first Title IX complaints to work its way into the court system, *Alexander v. Yale* (1980), did that work.[2] A sequence of large jury awards to plaintiffs in the early 2000s gave Title IX violations an important role in the articulation of a campus's sense of risk and legal exposure (e.g., in 2008, $19.1 million was awarded to a coach of the Fresno State women's basketball team; a judge reduced that award to $6.6 million).[3] Once associated in the public's mind almost exclusively with women's sports, Title IX is now a container for the conflicts and anxieties that shape how students, staff, and faculty understand their relationships to each other and to the institution.[4] Its administration is an important historical force: it is a major condition of possibility for the confrontation with institutionalized sexism, homophobia, and transphobia—much contemporary antitrans legislation in the United States can be understood as an attack on Title IX and as a response to advances made under its aegis (e.g., Title IX prohibits discrimination against trans athletes). But its administration can also be a vector through which bias announces itself. On a campus, the sense of what Title IX is may be expressed by person's ideas about what "the basis of sex" means. The committees charged with addressing these forms of harm are often populated by people who don't believe harassment is real. As is the case with juries: many—perhaps even most—people handling cases on our campuses are not experts in sexed and gendered forms of harm, and, if they are, they work in a context in which their expertise is likely undervalued.

Somewhat perversely, I think of Title IX as a formal articulation of a wish—a wish for a school in which sex is not a vector for shame, punishment, and social abjection. Title IX regulation describes an evolving sense of the least a school can do to make such a world possible. On most of our campuses, however, an administrative apparatus lifts the responsibility of enforcing that minimum from especially a faculty community who would prefer to assign the reproductive labor of working through sex-based forms of harm to a small group of socially abjected service workers. Faculty groan about "sex bureaucrats" ruining the school while avoiding opportunities to engage their community in the reproductive labor of tending to complaints about especially their own conduct.[5]

Title IX has become a symbolic dumping ground, a figure holding our collective sense of subjectification to the institution. We binge on stories of sexual shame and professional failure, stories of sexual violation, witch hunts, tribunals, and retribution. We flow from rumor-mongering threads on social media and blogs to op-eds about student paranoia and feminism run amok to news headlines announcing the exposure of one predator, then another, then another. Every rumor in this world feels true and every accusation feels false until something breaks. The shape of this discourse is itself harassing.

But people who file complaints are not thinking of this. I know I wasn't when I composed my first complaint. I thought that complaint would help stop my student from harassing me. I filed a second when I understood more about the administration of complaints: the focus of that complaint was the complaint process itself. I had hoped it might force the campus to address problems in the status of Title IX investigations and that it might address the problems created by faculty who used my scholarship and what they thought they knew about my sex life to absolve N of harassment. It did neither. But by the time I filed that second complaint, I understood the process as what Joseph Beuys described as social sculpture. The complaint created a situation, and that was the most I could do.

Sexual harassment cases body forth the contradiction of the disavowals that ground our understandings of work and school. The complainant pulls to the surface that which the institution must disavow: the school is a form of sexual community. "Institutions survive the stage of being fragile conventions," Mary Douglas writes, by reproducing the sense that "they are founded in nature and therefore, in reason."[6] These "founding analogies" style our thought about institutions and institutional life—and, Douglas argues, they work only to the extent that they are unacknowledged, hidden, even secret. Sex, she writes, appears as one such "natural" ground for institutional stability. This is certainly true for the university. The organization of the relationship between our work and our sexual lives is a key framework through which we understand what a good job supports: the ability to, say, own a home and start a family. It is parental leave, spousal benefits; it is also the explicit prohibition of sex with subordinate coworkers and the implicit sexualization of subordinate bodies. It is the management of that prohibition and the ritualization of violations of those rules. A sense of sex shapes what is recognized as teachable and not teachable; it shapes what is recognized as researchable and unknowable. The gendered foundation of success in the academy bubbles up to the surface of especially faculty resistance to antiharassment work precisely because antiharassment activism confronts the forms of sexual entitlement that feel, for some, like earned professional privilege if not sexuality itself. The antiharassment intervention does not expel sex from the workplace: it interrupts the disavowal of the fact that it is always already there. It can become an occasion for staging that disavowal.

The event of sexualized harassment and abuse can plug your body into an institutional power grid. Harassment moves through us in waves of dread, anxiety, grief, and alarm. We file complaints when we can't tolerate this state. Those who can will back away from harassment—harassment is sticky; speaking out about a harassment case can draw harassment into your life. Bullying and harassment work only where a majority of people will choose to minimize and ignore rather than engage and resist these toxic behaviors—this requires an openness to self-examination. Without that commitment, conversations and debates staged around stories of violation can escalate and amplify harassment dynamics—carrying harassment dynamics beyond a case's primary scene to Facebook walls, Twitter threads, and into the basement of unmoderated or barely moderated comments amplifying the hits for blog posts and tabloid-style reporting. The energies of violation, dread, anxiety, and anger detach from the people within a case. They become abstractions—accuser and accused become reversible; the truth of an individual case feels unknowable—we sink into this sense of sexual violation and sexual harassment as subjective, as unverifiable. Harassment itself comes to feel both pervasive and somehow unreal.

In this chapter, I think with one complaint filed against Larry Nassar in 2014 by Amanda Thomashow. At that time, Nassar was on the faculty at Michigan State University's College of Osteopathic Medicine and a clinician at the university's Sports Medicine clinic. Thomashow had gone to Nassar seeking treatment for hip pain; she accused him of assaulting her. The school's assistant director for institutional equity, Kristine Moore, cleared Nassar of wrongdoing. I am most interested in the July 18, 2014, memo summarizing that investigation and its findings. This is the document that was given to Thomashow to close her case; it is the result of her complaint.

Larry Nassar molested hundreds of girls and women over three decades. Less than four years after MSU dismissed Thomashow's complaint, he was sentenced to prison for the rest of his life. I am interested in what made the truth of Thomashow's complaint so difficult to accept. So is Thomashow. For years, she asked MSU to reopen that investigation, to look harder at what happened and how it happened. In their negotiations with the university, Nassar's other victims also asked for this, and for an apology from campus leadership for their failures. The university gave them $500 million but offered no apology that admitted to any wrongdoing on the university's part and made no commitment to examining the failure to respond appropriately to Thomashow's complaint. As of this writing, the university's discourse about Nassar has centered on his singular monstrosity—trustees, for example, are sorry that so many were abused by him.[7] They are not sorry, at least not officially, for their own complicity in the institutional culture that enabled him.

Writing about actual cases is a challenge. Casual engagement with especially unresolved or poorly resolved cases risks contributing to the harassment dynamics internal to the case's impacted communities. Larry Nassar's abuse of his patients, however, has been addressed in a mind-boggling number of news articles, blog posts, and podcasts and in television coverage. The case grew out of a series of long-form investigative reports on sexual abuse in sports.[8] Victim testimony is readily available, as are court documents, Title IX reports, police reports, and court filings related to the numerous lawsuits against, for example, MSU and USA Gymnastics. We have access to an unusually rich, detailed multimedia archive documenting the experiences of Nassar's victims, police investigation of complaints, and institutional responses to them. Given the scale of material out there, I feel confident that my writing is not harmful.[9] I make this point because in my field, the highest-profile writing about actual cases has been quite harmful.[10]

Writing about this case requires that I address some of my rhetorical decisions. I privilege the word *victim*, for example, over *survivor* throughout this essay. I draw frequently from statements made by Nassar's victims and their families as recorded by journalists and in police reports and court filings. This is, in essence, a trigger warning—I need to share what Nassar did through the explicit language used by victims because this essay reflects on and pushes back against the representation of the victims in this case as unknowing, sexually innocent, and, in Thomashow's case, hysterical. I have tried to avoid trafficking in the sensational economy of harassment narratives, but my aims require being frank. If I prefer the word *victim* in this context, it is because my focus here is not on the recovery and survival experiences of the people he harmed, but on the scene of their disenfranchisement as subjects with the capacity to understand, know, and represent what was happening to their own bodies. This essay focuses on a context in which victims are overwhelmingly cisgendered girls and women and in which the abuser is a cisgendered man. Much of what I say here is likely to resonate, however, with gender-nonconforming, genderqueer, nonbinary, and trans readers. This story revolves around profound violations staged within a medical context: far too many readers will have had some experience of sexed and gendered harm within their health care. The Nassar case is not as extraordinary as it seems: cases involving hundreds of people victimized by doctors or physical therapists have surfaced at the University of Southern California, the University of California, Los Angeles, Ohio State University, and at a community clinic run by Johns Hopkins University. I hope my writing functions as a hazmat suit that allows readers to enter this scene of violation without being dismantled by the subject.

First, some context. In 2014, MSU's campus community was deeply engaged in conversation and debate about the problem of sexual violence and sexual harassment. That year, a case of sexual violence and relational abuse at MSU had opened a *Harper's Magazine* article, "Ending College Sexual Assault."[11] Local news outlets routinely covered the university's struggles with cases of sexual violence, including high-profile accusations against student athletes. The campus newspaper featured stories about badly handled complaints, op-eds from students describing their experiences with sexual harassment, and updates on policy revision and on campus activism. Anti–sexual violence and antiharassment activists at MSU were part of a national movement that has its roots in Title IX's passage in 1972 but which gained momentum, especially in 2013 when students at UNC Chapel Hill founded a knowledge-sharing network that empowers students to engage administrative processes to address the problem of sexual harassment and sexual assault (End Rape on Campus). That group worked with student complainants at MSU; they succeeded in pressuring the Department of Education to investigate the university's compliance with Title IX requirements in the adjudication of sex-based complaints.[12] In 2014, when Thomashow filed her complaint, MSU was in the middle of that investigative process.[13] It was one of dozens of schools across the country then under investigation and in the news. Joan W. Howarth, dean of MSU Law through the period of the federal investigation of the campus, writes that during this period MSU "faced heavy pressure from the Department of Education, and in some sense that pressure transformed the campus, with new university resources, overhaul of the Title IX regimen, new and visible student activism, and hypersensitivity to Title IX procedural compliance."[14] Sexual violence was addressed at the campus's Spring Break

Safety Fair. In that year, MSU's administration instituted new mandatory reporting guidelines. In April, the campus launched No Excuse for Sexual Assault, an awareness program that addressed myths about rape and educated students about the meaning of consent.[15] Volunteers raised awareness about sexual assault in residence halls, and the campus hosted "male panels on rape culture," a candlelight vigil, film screenings, and more. In the fall, university president Lou Anna Simon announced the campus's participation in It's on Us, a rape awareness campaign initiated by the White House. A celebrity-packed public service announcement was played at home football games—this fact was lauded in an article posted on the White House blog.[16] Administrators, students, staff, and faculty at MSU were, in other words, fully dialed into the work of addressing sex-based violence and harassment within their community.

Given this, many were shocked by the university's decision to invite George Will to give a commencement address at the campus's December ceremony. In June of that year, Will had published an op-ed in the *Washington Post* that denounced antiharassment/anti–sexual violence activists and administrators as oversensitive ideologues. He argued that these administrators and activists were "making everyone hypersensitive, even delusional, about victimizations." Students and faculty at MSU were outraged by his selection as a graduation speaker and as the recipient of an honorary degree. Their anger was concentrated on how Will described sexual assault victims. He argued that the current turn to the problem of sexual harassment and sexual assault on college campuses makes "victimhood a coveted status that confers privileges" and that, as it does so, "victims proliferate."[17]

Will has been a vocal critic of Title IX for years: before his attention turned to the subject of sexual assault, he often warned that Title IX would be the death of men's sports and railed against "Title IX imperialists" who want to extend its administrative reach "from locker rooms to classrooms."[18] It seems likely that Will was selected as a commencement speaker precisely because he was (and is) a high-profile figure in conversations about Title IX and campus culture and because the MSU community was engaged in conversation and debate about Title IX compliance. Although speakers were announced less than two weeks before the ceremony, nearly seventy thousand people signed a petition protesting Will's selection. Students staged a sit-in in the president's office. The Council of Graduate Students passed a resolution condemning the invitation. The General Assembly for the campus undergraduate student government voted by a very strong majority to condemn the choice and asked the university administration to allocate the amount paid him ($47,500) to support victims of sexual assault.[19] Simon responded to this by lecturing student activists on the importance of academic debate. At the graduation ceremony, when Will got up to speak, some students turned their backs to him. Other students staged an alternate ceremony.[20]

The university invited two other distinguished figures to give commencement addresses that month, the filmmaker Michael Moore and Teresa Sullivan. Sullivan, an MSU alumna, was then president of the University of Virginia. At the time, her campus was roiling in response to the scandal of a sensationalist *Rolling Stone* exposé of a gang rape at a fraternity that, it turned out, was spectacularly poor reporting on a false accusation.[21] That story was published in November and retracted in early December, not two weeks before her MSU address. By the close of 2014, the subject of false accusations saturated the already intense discourse on campus sexual assault.

Will's take on Title IX and campus harassment is typical of punditry that narrates the issue of sexual harassment as a crisis manufactured by fragile, hysterical students and crusading feminists scrambling for bureaucratic authority. In one think piece after another, Amanda Hess writes, college students have been represented as "whiny, entitled products of helicopter parenting and participation trophies."[22] Greg Lukianodd and Jonathan Heidt, in their 2015 essay "The Coddling of the American Mind," warn that students are increasingly thin-skinned, encouraged in their sense of their individual and collective vulnerability by an institutional culture invested in "vindictive protectiveness." Much discourse about Title IX represents this piece of legislation as itself a seducer, luring students into imagining themselves as rape victims and instituting a "neo-Victorian" era.[23] In this narrative, drunken naïfs meet the machine of government overreach—the administrative apparatus of Title IX bears down on the campus, offering itself to inexperienced youngsters like a morning-after pill.[24] Emily Yoffe, for example, warned that "under the worthy mandate of protecting victims of sexual assault, procedures are being put in place at colleges that presume the guilt of the accused."[25] Over a period of two years, Yoffe would go on to write a series of op-eds for *Slate* and the *Atlantic* elaborating on this issue, moving smoothly from a critique of alarmist presentations of the campus as a hunting ground to sounding the alarm on behalf of the falsely accused and advising women to avoid drinking too much as a rape-prevention strategy. *New York Times* columnist Ross Douthat joins this chorus of the concerned by observing, "It is very hard for anyone, including the young women and young men involved, to figure out what distinguishes a real assault from a bad or gross or swiftly regretted consensual encounter."[26] In this story, the Title IX administrator arrives on the scene as an ideological predator, exploiting the situation of desire to trick students out of their confusion and into complaint. Under liberalism's pressure, Douthat warns, "the rule of pleasure gives way to the rule of secret tribunals and Title IX administrators."[27] The problem, in these narratives, is that the law can never be adequate to the messiness of sexual desire. Thus Laura Kipnis, in her widely read and discussed *Unwanted Advances*, describes today's students as initiating a "culture of sexual paranoia . . . so effectively dumbing down the place that the traditional idea of the university—as a refuge for complexity, a setting for the free exchange of ideas—is getting buried under an avalanche of platitudes and fear."[28]

Discourse on the sexual politics of the campus toggles between warnings that the campus is a "hunting ground" (e.g., Dick Kirby's film of that name) populated by sexual predators and laments that the campus is overrun by hysterics who confuse bad sex and rape and are happy to sacrifice academic freedom to the altar of their delicate feelings (e.g. Kipnis, Yoffe). We have a national, student-led anti–sexual violence movement, and cries of scholars and pundits who fear that the application of Title IX to the administration of sexual life on campus will come at the cost of academic freedom and our collective sexual happiness. In 2014, the MSU community was very much living in the space between these narratives.

In giving this selective overview of discourse on campus sexual harassment, I have deliberately staged an ugly irony. On March 24, 2014, in this year of change and debate about sexual harassment and Title IX administration, Amanda Thomashow went to see Larry Nassar for treatment for pain related to injuries that she had accrued as an athlete. He had a good reputation and was treating her younger sister. During Thomashow's office visit, Nassar made a strange remark about how "her boyfriend needed to give her better massages."[29] He sent his assistant out of the room and began to molest her. He "cupped her buttocks, massaged her breasts and vaginal area."[30] He had reached under her shirt and bra to grope her breast, she explained, like someone would if they were "making out with you" (3). He reached under her clothes and underwear and began to massage her "vaginal area" (4), moving three fingers in a circle. He was not wearing gloves and gave no explanation for what he was doing. "She was shocked" (4). She told him to stop. He said he wasn't finished. He was "'extremely close' to inserting a finger into her vagina."[31] She stood up and physically pushed him off her body. She observed that he was visibly aroused.[32] He would not let her leave the room until she promised to come back for, as she put it, "a follow-up assault."[33] She later canceled the next appointment Nassar had insisted on scheduling; she told his assistant that "she was cancelling because she felt violated" (5). On April 18, she contacted another doctor on staff at MSU and lodged a complaint.[34] The university's office charged with handling Title IX complaints ran an investigation regarding the question of whether or not Nassar had sexually assaulted her. That investigation cleared him.

Nassar did not dispute her account of the session. While he claimed not to remember the details of their session, he told investigators that "Ms. Thomashow's description sounds like standard operating procedure" (9). The investigator's findings pivoted on the conclusion that Amanda Thomashow did not understand the "nuanced difference" between a medical procedure and sexual assault; the report excludes key elements of Thomashow's narrative, including the fact that she had to push Nassar off her and also that she had observed that he had an erection.

Quite rightly, media coverage of this case makes much of the report's use of the term "nuanced difference." It has always struck me as odd; it is a strange way of describing the difference between a medical treatment and sexual assault. Moore uses the phrase in a confusing section of the report covering her interviews with four of Nassar's colleagues. These colleagues were consulted as "physicians and treating professionals in this area" who could evaluate the professionalism of his conduct. All of them were women. The three who were practicing osteopaths and therapists said they would not massage a patient underneath her clothing (as was Nassar's practice). Brooke Lemmen, a student of Nassar's and a "good friend," said that "she does not touch under the shirt because she is sensitive to that issue, as a woman" (12). Questioned about Nassar's reaching under Thomashow's underpants, she explained that "she would not use a skin-on-skin method, she would go over clothes in part because she is sensitive to what that would mean for the patient" (13). Dr. Lisa DeStefano, a classmate and colleague of Nassar's, was described by Moore as making a nearly identical statement regarding her own practice when treating intimate zones of the body. She explained that while there might be benefits to skin-on-skin massage, "as a woman, she is sensitive to the fact that skin-to-skin contact may be uncomfortable to some" (15). Dr. Jennifer Gilmore also testified that, as a matter of "personal preference," she massaged patients over their clothes when using the technique Nassar claimed to be performing. Nassar's practice of reaching under patient's clothing (and without gloves) is shrugged off by all three interviewees and by the investigator. Within the report, these interviewees are presented as having an understanding, as women, of patient vulnerability that Nassar, as a man, does not. This difference is framed as a difference in sex, rather than one of professionalism.

In this section of the report, Moore goes on to enact a substitution of massage for assault; this displaces the actual nature of Thomashow's complaint. As Nassar's colleagues explain why they do not massage underneath their patients' clothing, they nod to their patients' sense of boundaries. Moore narrates these decisions as made to avoid confusion between therapeutic manipulation and massage, even though it is clear that the potential for confusion addressed by these women is one in which a patient might feel not massaged but violated.

Nassar claimed to be working on Thomashow's sacrotuberous ligament (located in the lower and back part of the pelvis). Gilmore explains that when she performs this kind of release, she tells patients, "I will be right by your butt-bone" (17); DeStefano describes using her fingers on the patient's buttocks (15). In her summary of her interview with DeStefano, Moore writes "that this type of manipulation, which is medically appropriate, could be confused with massage" (15). In a note, Moore addresses the fuzzy language used across the report when referring to this area of the body—"the layperson's understanding of the vaginal area could include the 'underwear zone.' When using the term 'vagina area,' [Dr. Lemmen] is talking about palpation outside of the labia" (13). In the report's conclusion, Moore casts this distinction between massage and manipulation, and between vagina, labia, and "underwear zone," as the crux of the problem: "The STL (sacrotuberous ligament) is very close to the vaginal area. Manipulation or palpation can be interpreted as massage to someone who is not familiar with osteopathic medicine and would not know the nuanced difference between the two" (19). One might consider the difference between massage and manipulation to be "nuanced"; the difference that Thomashow was drawing, however, was between a therapeutic, medical practice and sexual assault. It is also very hard to imagine that Thomashow was confused about the difference between her vagina, labia, and underwear zone, and, furthermore, that this confusion would lead her to mistake massage for assault. Across this relatively brief document (it is barely twenty-two pages), this kind of confusion seems to strike the interviewer and Nassar's witnesses as more plausible than the possibility that Thomashow knew exactly what she was talking about when she reported that Nassar was "extremely close to inserting a finger into her vaginal opening" (4). That language is actually quite grounded and specific, unlike the language used by nearly everyone else cited in the report.

The language of the report's conclusion is confusing on another score. Moore legitimizes Thomashow's experience of Nassar's behavior as harassing and yet concludes that she was not harassed. She writes, "the trauma suffered by [Thomashow] is deeply felt and not short term" (22). Moore contextualizes that trauma with Nassar's failure to explain what he was doing: "Without adequate knowledge about this procedure and without choice related to the procedure, a reasonable person could feel shock, shame, embarrassment and violated." Her trauma, in other words, is reasonable. This is important because reasonableness is a key term in definitions of sexual harassment. As Moore explains, "A person's subjective belief that behavior is offensive does not make that behavior sexual harassment. That behavior must also be objectively unreasonable" (19). That Nassar touched a sexual part of Thomashow's body without her consent is not in dispute; that Moore found that a "reasonable person could feel shock" in response to Nassar's conduct could have supported a harassment complaint. Moore, assuming that Nassar did not, in fact, try to insert a finger into Thomashow's vaginal opening, focuses instead on whether his touching of her "underwear area" was sexual for Nassar—and on whether Thomashow was capable of understanding what he was doing.

Every signature of a sexual assault is present in Thomashow's account. Nassar groped her; he began trying to penetrate her. She asked him to stop; he refused. She physically pushed him off her body. She told the receptionist that she felt "violated." She was not confused about what happened. Her narrative, as well as those of her friends, family, and colleagues, is clear and consistent. Moore might have concluded that she was unable to decide on the charge's validity. Nassar had, after all, sent his assistant out of the room. Instead, she decides that Thomashow was wrong. "The touching," she writes, "was medically appropriate," and "so none of these factors [e.g., the absence of informed consent] create a hostile environment," as defined by school policy: "We cannot find that the conduct was of a sexual nature. Thus, it did not violate the Sexual Harassment Policy. However, we find the claim helpful in that it allows us to examine certain practices at the MSU Sports Medicine Clinic" (22). In essence, Moore found that Thomashow had sexualized the interaction, not Nassar.

Four years after this report was written, following a cascade of criminal complaints and lawsuits filed in courts in Michigan, California, and Texas,

Larry Nassar pled guilty to criminal sexual abuse charges. He was sentenced to prison for the rest of his life. Michigan State University agreed to a $500 million settlement with over three hundred victims of the sexual abuse that he doled out while working at MSU and which he presented to his patients, if he bothered to explain it at all, as pelvic floor therapy. There are many more victims, of course: there are all the people he abused while working for USA Gymnastics. The fallout from this case is still rippling across sports.

Today, when we look at the 2014 report and its conclusion, we gasp in astonishment: How could the people receiving this complaint not have known what Nassar was doing?[35] The 2014 report that cleared Larry Nassar is a stunning example of what philosopher Miranda Fricker theorizes as "epistemic injustice," where a "wrong is done to someone specifically in their capacity as a knower."[36] Fricker's writing on epistemic injustice takes up two vectors of this form of harm. "Testimonial injustice" describes the impact of the bias that renders a person's word meaningless. "Hermeneutical injustice" describes "a gap in collective interpretive resources [that] puts someone at an unfair disadvantage when it comes to making sense of their social experience."[37] In Fricker's work, sexual harassment cases are of paradigmatic importance for understanding the nature of hermeneutical injustice insofar as they often manifest how "extant collective hermeneutical resources can have a lacuna where the name of a distinctive social experience should be."[38] Thus, victims of harassment may struggle to find the language to describe, make sense of, and respond to their experiences. Fricker's examination of the overdetermination of problems of knowing with regard to sexual harassment echoes the work of other feminist theorists of sex, violence, and agency. Sharon Marcus argues, for example, that "a feminist politics which would fight rape" requires more than "developing a language about rape"; it requires "understanding rape to be a language."[39] Sex-based forms of violence are presented as an "inevitable material fact of life."[40] Within this "gendered grammar of violence," the category *woman* is marked as "always already rapeable."[41] "What founds these languages," Marcus explains, "are neither real nor objective criteria, but political decisions to exclude certain interpretations and perspectives and to privilege others."[42] Marcus does not argue that rape is "merely" discursive. She situates sexualized forms of violence within a material practice of disenfranchisement. That practice expresses itself in law, in language, and in the body. It shapes our sense of the thinkable and the speakable.

Knowledge problems collect around sexual violence. For example, a cultural reinforcement of the relationship between sexual assault and trauma positions the rape victim as an inherently bad witness. The rape victim, in the discourse of rape, is trapped within what Jan Jordan theorized as "the credibility conundrum."[43] She is either traumatized and therefore suffers from memory lapses, or she is not traumatized and therefore is not really a victim, because rape is, in the discourse of rape, always traumatic. The mapping of rape and trauma onto each other has all kinds of effects on what happens when victims speak about what happened to them. As Bianca Crewe and Jonathan Ichikawa write, "If, according to the available hermeneutics, the trauma of sexual assault damages a potential testifier specifically in terms of their capacities *qua* testifiers, then it will be impossible for their testimony to convey knowledge."[44] This conundrum expresses much more than the impact of trauma: it is the product of an ideological system that alienates victims from the social mechanisms through which we understand what is true. This issue has been taken up by feminist critics over the decades—it's a defining aspect of feminist writing about sexual knowledge and sexual assault. The precondition for this crisis of knowing is the sexual subject's status as always already violated, always already traumatized—she is the embodiment of a truth problem.

The difficulty of Thomashow's position as a witness to her own violation resonates with the contradictions surrounding the discourse of rape. Investigators for MSU affirmed that Thomashow's feelings (anger, betrayal, shock) were reasonable ("a reasonable person could feel shock"). Although the report affirms that Thomashow suffered trauma, the investigator decided that she was traumatized not by her doctor's betrayal of her trust but by what she did not know. The trauma invoked in the language of the report's conclusion unfolds in the domain of the always-already described by Marcus—a baseline state of sexualized vulnerability that is coincident with having, in essence, the wrong kind of sexual knowledge. Her shock is framed as a woman's natural reaction to a man approaching this part of her body. Her response is sexual; his action is not. Within the report, furthermore, the witnesses for accuser and accused are drawn from their personal circles of friends and colleagues. Of Thomashow's four witnesses, at least two are health care professionals. One of those two worked with Nassar. In the report, she says that Nassar's behavior, as described by Thomashow, "sounds extremely inappropriate." She refers to a woman whose daughter had been treated by Nassar at her workplace; that woman "had been very uncomfortable with what [Nassar] did to her daughter" (8). Another interviewee described Nassar as "creepy and goofy" and said that she would not see him again. All of Thomashow's witnesses are presented in the report as friends and family; the report does not record any sustained engagement with their understanding of the professionalism of the behavior described by Thomashow. All of Nassar's witnesses were his friends and colleagues. All four are presented in the report as experts, and their observations on this point guide the writing in the report.

Thomashow is furthermore structurally positioned as the subject of the investigation and not as, say, a member of the community of readers to whom the investigative report is addressed. This is not unusual, but in this case MSU actually produced two versions of the investigative report—one shared with Thomashow, and another written for MSU officials. The conclusion for the latter report is longer and explicitly identifies Nassar's behavior as dangerous for the institution: "We find that whether medically sound or not, the failure to adequately explain procedures such as these invasive, sensitive procedures, is opening the practice up to liability and is exposing patients to unnecessary trauma based on the possibility of perceived inappropriate sexual conduct. In addition, we find that the failure to obtain consent from patients prior to the procedure is likewise exposing the practice to liability."[45] This in-house report separates the question of the professionalism of Nassar's practice (even regarding something as basic as informing patients about the treatment he claimed to be offering) from the question of "inappropriate sexual conduct," reducing the difference between the two to a matter of perception regarding the nature of his touch. It seems to have occurred to no one at MSU that professional misconduct might also be sexual misconduct, and that this misconduct might include not only touching but a failure to adhere to the most basic protocols used in addressing especially intimate parts of the body. In keeping with this, Moore's report does not address Thomashow's observations regarding Nassar's joke about her boyfriend needing to give her better massages and the testimony of witnesses who describe Nassar's behavior toward other patients as "creepy." The report reinforces the implicit, commonsense positioning of sexual and professional misconduct as separate issues, while reinforcing a contradictory normalization of overt sexism within professional life (and so the boyfriend joke is just talk).

Hermeneutical and testimonial forms of injustice mirror and amplify each other when sexual harassment cases land in the hands of people who are deeply uncomfortable with any direct discussion of sex and sexuality. Nassar assumed the mantle of sexual knowledge for his community; that community deferred to him and trusted his assertion that what he was doing was not sexual. The 2014 report clearing Nassar is just one manifestation of the negation of the complaints girls and women (nearly all of whom were athletes seeking treatment for injuries) had been staging within their training and coaching relationships, within friendships, athletic departments and teams, and within complaint systems.[46] Athletes who complained about Nassar, who disclosed but who did not file official complaints, describe feeling "crazy," especially as the people around them participated in a group gaslighting, tagging them as "whores" and leaving them feeling that it was they who had sexualized their experience of Nassar's "treatments."[47] In 1997, MSU gymnast Larissa Boyce told her coach Kathie Klages that Nassar was molesting her. Klages convinced her that Boyce was "misunderstanding it" and discouraged Boyce from reporting, even though a second athlete had come forward with an identical complaint. She was asked to apologize to Nassar, and did. To demonstrate to her coaches that she did not have a "dirty mind," she submitted herself to more "treatments."[48] In 2011, after a particularly abusive session, national team gymnast McKayla Maroney told her coach, "Last night it was like Larry was fingering me." That disclosure, witnessed by three other athletes, was met with silence.[49]

The narratives of Nassar's victims take on the form of crises of knowing—of feeling stupid/not stupid—a feeling that also revolves around the difficulty of squaring their sense of what was happening with the shame of being the subject who names his conduct as sexual. Rachael Denhollander (the first victim to come forward publicly) told investigators that she "felt stupid for not knowing better."[50] She responded to her sense that something was wrong by educating herself about pelvic floor physiotherapy. Kamerin Moore was so plagued by injury that she became Nassar's "guinea pig." "I don't blame myself," she testified, "for being the innocent child that I was."[51] In 2004, Brianne Randall Gay told police she "was 'scared' and 'uncomfortable'" when Nassar, during an appointment to treat back pain, massaged her breasts and "placed his hand on her bare vagina." She "didn't know if it was possible that this type of touching was normal in this type of doctor visit," so she told her mother, who called the police. The police dropped the investigation after talking to Nassar. Nassar had shared a slide presentation on the biomechanics of the sacrotuberous ligament—no element of that presentation explains why he would place a hand directly on a patient's genitals or grope and squeeze her breasts.[52] Investigators in that case never discussed his treatment practice with professionals. At Nassar's sentencing, the mother of "victim 105" testified that when she questioned him about the fact that he was not using gloves when he penetrated her daughter, Nassar "made me feel stupid for asking. I told myself, 'He's an Olympic doctor. Be quiet.'" Another victim: "I was unaware not because I was naive but because I was a child."[53] National team gymnast Jordyn Wieber testified that "the worst part is that I had no idea that he was sexually abusing me. . . . I knew it felt strange . . . but he was the national team doctor." She talked with her teammates: "None of us really understood it." "I am angry with myself for not recognizing the abuse."[54] Numbers of his victims describe Nassar giving them orgasms; they were so young and inexperienced that they didn't understand what was happening to them.

Amanda Thomashow, as she explained in a statement delivered at Nassar's sentencing, was not a child "without the words to explain what he did. I was a woman in my mid 20s, studying at a medical school and working at a pediatrician's office. I knew he had abused me."[55] During the investigation of Thomashow's 2014 complaint, when researching his so-called medical practice, MSU officials spoke only to people who had close ties to Nassar. Brooke Lemmen, in fact, would later move patient files at his request when he was under another investigation.[56] When MSU's police department investigated Thomashow's complaint, Nassar told detectives that he was a "body whisperer." He offered to demonstrate his technique on a volunteer, said he "wasn't a deviant," and, as evidence of this, explained that he didn't even have sex until his honeymoon: "That's the essence of who I am."[57] His description of his practice is, on its face, creepy: "Most of the time my eyes are closed. . . . Use the force, you feel it. . . . It is a conceptual thing. It is you, the patient, and the spirit."[58] During the MSU investigation, Nassar shared a PowerPoint presentation that he used to explain his practice. One slide featured an image drawn from *Star Trek* and was titled "Pelvic floor: Where no man has gone before."[59] Again, these statements are from Nassar himself, submitted as evidence of his professionalism.

Reading available materials related to investigations of Nassar, it becomes clear that the people running them knew less about the physiology of the pelvic region than his victims. They seem, to me, eager to let Nassar do the explaining for them—his defenses of himself are incoherent and contradictory, and this is what people, when listening to sex talk, expect. It is as if, in these investigations, the pelvis itself were cordoned off as beyond investigation—as if this part of the body were beyond knowing ("where no man has gone before"). Those who tried to talk about the abuse had to argue for not only their reasonableness but for something even more basic—for their awareness, their consciousness, for an intentional relationship to their bodies. They needed to map the relationship of one part of the body (genitals, breasts) to another (hips, back, shoulders, neck). They argued against the metonymic substitution of the vagina for their entire being, and lost.

It is worth pausing to discuss the treatment that Nassar claimed to be offering. In Thomashow's case, Nassar claimed to be working on the sacrotuberous ligament (the release of which can require working on a patient's backside, near the coccyx); in other instances, in which he was penetrating his patients, he described his actions as "pelvic floor therapy." Pelvic floor physiotherapy is not included in standard training and certification for physical therapists.[60] It is a specialization. Pelvic floor physiotherapy is usually given to people who suffer from incontinence and/or painful intercourse and may be used for hip and low back pain.[61] It does have benefits for athletes, and for men.[62] Patients tend to be older than the athletes Nassar treated—American Physical Therapy Association guidelines,[63] in fact, are clear regarding its inappropriateness for young children and for people who have never had a gynecological exam. Some of the symptoms addressed by this treatment (e.g., uterine prolapse, urinary incontinence) are more prevalent in older people and in people who have given birth. These are, furthermore, not uncommon ailments—the treatment, in fact, is not as rare as discourse in coverage of this case would suggest. Patients are referred to specialists, and standard practice is to align the therapist's and patient's gender and for the patient to be heavily involved in conversations about the treatment and its protocols. Informed consent is solicited with every treatment and should be reaffirmed (and can be withdrawn) during a session.[64] Literature on the subject stresses the importance of this nonsurgical, nonpharmaceutical treatment for common debilitating and humiliating ailments and the necessity for the development of professional guidelines to prevent not only sexual abuse but traumatization of patients. The importance of this latter issue is amplified by a number of studies that link pelvic dysfunction to histories of sexual abuse.[65]

So much shame clings to this part of the human anatomy that many patients seek this therapy only as a last resort.[66] Misogyny and sexism, racism, and homo- and transphobia target this part of the body. Pelvic floor physiotherapy addresses the only horizontal load-bearing muscle complex in the standing body—a muscle group that supports a sense of containment, of bodily integrity. How many of us who practice yoga have been undone by the emotion released in poses that address this part of the body? Pelvic floor work is personal and political body work. People investigating complaints against

Nassar shrugged off the absence of basic professional protocols in a practice that is, perhaps, of all forms of physiotherapy, the one around which there is, in the profession, the most intense awareness of patient vulnerability.

Nassar's packaging of the sexual abuse of his patients as pelvic massage therapy has a recognizable medical history that serves to normalize the vulnerability of the patient. Modern gynecology's origins are in abuse: grisly experimentation on enslaved women, forced medical exams on women identified as prostitutes and disease vectors.[67] The examination of women's sex parts is also baked into sports institutions in the form of sex-segregated athletic competition, a structure that can only be produced in and through sexualized forms of abuse and violence.[68] In 1966, the International Olympic Committee required mandatory evaluation of the genitals of women athletes.[69] A few years later this ugly ritual (which could be staged as a parade of athletes before doctors, or close individual inspection) was replaced by a chromosome test. That test produced its own problems and has since been replaced by another miserable process, centered on hormone levels and racist, sexist, and homophobic standards of gender normativity. Once identified as embodying a gender problem (often by competitors or by athletic officials), these athletes are subjected to hormone tests and a "protocol [that] involves measuring and palpating the clitoris, vagina and labia, as well as evaluating breast size and pubic hair scored on an illustrated five-grade scale."[70] Today, a handful of women from the global south are hunted by teams of creepy doctors and sports officials, intent on running them out of the category *woman*. It is not a stretch to say that the whole of women's sports is haunted by sexual violence. Athletes today are fighting policies that require them to subject themselves to unnecessary medical interventions, including surgery, to bring their bodies into compliance with arbitrary standards of gender difference based on junk science.[71]

All of the forms of violence I describe in the previous paragraph have been framed in terms of care and protection (e.g., the protection of women from disease, the protection of fairness in sports). Sameena Mulla, in her analysis of the entanglement of care and violence in the scene of sexual assault intervention, offers important insight regarding the way that traditions of care can enforce an alienation from one's sexual body, especially as one turns to an institution for help. Mulla's close reading of postassault treatment of victims receiving care in a Baltimore emergency room surfaces a number of practices that might support our understanding of what happened to Nassar's victims. Traditionally, for example, during pelvic exams an apron is draped over a patient's bent legs, separating person from pelvis as well as patient from doctor. I quote Mulla at some length, because her observations are important for understanding the space of the encounter between Nassar and his victims:

> The potential intimacy and awkwardness of performing a pelvic examination are mitigated by a process of objectification. That is, a distinction between the patient as person and as a pelvis are rigorously maintained in the way that gazes are mediated. In many traditions of gynecological practice, the ideal patient is one who can shed her personhood while on the exam table and succumb to the transformation of person into a pelvis. Gynecological professionalism demands that during the examination, practitioners orient toward their patient solely as a pelvis. Thus, a gynecologist will encourage the use of a drape or robe that isolates the patient's genitals, and while the patient is in the lithotomy position [in stirrups], she will ignore face-to-face interactions and will rarely maintain eye contact with the patient, even when she is addressing the patient. The patient, in turn, does not subject the practitioner to her gaze. Rather, she directs her eyes to some fixed point on the ceiling and responds to the practitioner's queries as though the pelvis under scrutiny is not her own.[72]

Nassar was not performing gynecological exams, and these protocols are actually not those of physiotherapy. But he could depend on the fact that even his youngest victims and (especially) their adult chaperones would have had a broad sense of the above-described practice of disassociation as, in essence, the requirements of being a good patient—especially when the doctor approaches one's genitals. This compliant patient agrees to interact indirectly with their caregiver through an abstracted, segmented body—an assemblage of parts. Nassar, according to statements made by a number of victims, often hid what he was doing from their sight lines (sometimes by using draping, sometimes by having victims change into baggy shorts, sometimes by positioning and approaching their bodies in a way that obscured their vision)—this was also how he hid his behavior from parents chaperoning treatment of their children. When alone with patients, Nassar sometimes engaged in sexual patter—layering chit-chat about massages, blow jobs, and boyfriends over his molestation of their bodies while pretending that he was giving them physical therapy. He did this to Thomashow when he joked that her boyfriend needed to give her better massages before groping her breast. In a very real sense, he presented himself as a friend to the girls and women he abused—verbally disavowing the power he exerted over the bodies of especially those who were required to be treated by Nassar while they competed as members of the USA national gymnastics squad or as members of MSU sports teams.

Mulla's analysis of the forensic encounter sheds additional light on other problems encountered in the history of complaints against Nassar. Standard to forensic examination of victims of sexual violence is the photographing of the victim's body. For a wide range of reasons, surprisingly little comes of these photographs—very few cases make it to a jury trial, and in those instances in which they do, prosecutors may avoid using them. Juries, Mulla explains, can be deeply uncomfortable with close-up photographs of a person's genitals. Showing that material can work against the victim's interests. Members of a jury cannot be counted on to understand the content of such images— they are unlikely to be familiar enough with them to recognize a wound, and they may experience a visceral repugnance that makes contemplating such images impossible. These images provoke shame and a desire to look away.[73] Many of the investigators who interviewed Nassar showed this level of discomfort: they put no pressure on his own explanations for what he was doing. For example, he claimed he was working near genitals but not on them or in them. But he also claimed to be an expert in pelvic massage therapy. He presented himself to his victims as an expert in pelvic floor work but, when interviewed by the police and by journalists in a later case, he said he had never received training in it. He denied penetrating his patients and routinely left the fact that he was doing so out of their medical records. The community of faculty and administrators at MSU might have responded to the evidence produced around Thomashow's complaint quite differently had they been willing to examine their own impulses to look away from the case and its details.

Title IX, as a tool, spotlights the place of sexual violation in the founding mythologies, archaic histories, and traditions that define the school. The fact that there are laws prohibiting sex-based discrimination, however, does not guarantee a good or fair outcome for a complaint. An investigation and disciplinary process has the capacity to ritualize something quite different: it may stage the articulation of an institution's mythology. It will produce the truth that the institution needs. An investigation may force an encounter with forms of unbearable knowledge—it may require a confrontation with not just the singular event of a violation but the ongoingness of the sexualized abuse of power in the everyday. One must work through the latter, unlearn one's unknowing, in order to grasp the truth of the former.

The narrative structures offered by a university's administrative culture can reproduce, amplify, nurture, and sustain the forms of incoherence that support the reproduction of sexualized forms of harm. The problem is not that most people are explicitly invested in reproducing sexual violence but that sexual violence and violation are grounding forces in our lives, and institutions present themselves as structures which regulate and manage that problem for us. This may be particularly true for the school, which carries us from early childhood through adolescence and into adulthood.[74] Within the institution, the need to understand and value what a person says about their experience with harassment is all too often deferred to a process, projected onto a structure of institutional authority. This yields a phenomenon that Félix Guattari described as "a fixed transference, a rigid mechanism, like the relationship of nurses and patients with the doctor, an obligatory, predetermined 'territorialised' transference onto a particular role or stereotype." For Guattari, this "is a way of interiorizing bourgeois repression by the repetitive, archaic, and artificial re-emergence of the phenomena of caste, with all the spell-binding and reactionary group phantasies they bring in their train."[75] Some antiharassment and antidiscrimination complaints cannot be addressed without breaking these cemented social forms that pattern (and limit) our work and our relationships to each other.

An institution, social structure, group, or organizational culture may be deeply invested in what Eve Kosofsky Sedgwick called "the privilege of unknowing"—the mythologies of these structures may, in fact, originate in profound forms of disavowal experienced by members of that institution as fundamentally necessary to the institution's well-being and to the individual's sense of order (and their place within it). "Knowledge," Sedgwick writes, "is not itself power; it is a magnetic field of power. Ignorance and opacity collude or compete with it in mobilizing the flows of energy, desire, goods, meanings, persons."[76] The Nassar case surfaces the proximity of knowingness and ignorance, innocence and shame where sex is concerned. Nassar's women colleagues, for example, knew how their patients felt when a doctor slid his ungloved hands underneath their panties. Nassar's privilege was that his colleagues were invested in the idea that he did not.

ALETHURGY'S SHADOWS

Truth-Telling between Women
in Elena Ferrante's *Neapolitan* Novels

In a series of lectures on truth-telling and government anchored by readings of classical drama, Michel Foucault uses the term *alethurgy* to name "the set of verbal procedures by which one brings to light that which is laid down as true as opposed to the false, hidden, inexpressible, unforeseen or forgotten."[1] He offers the following axiom: "There is no exercise of power without something like an alethurgy."[2]

We enter complaint processes with the hope that it will bring us this form of recognition and validation, a hope that is conditioned by attachments to the sense of what a court is and what it does, attachments we maintain even when working outside juridical structures. Foucault is interested in the alignment between governance and the ritual production of a fearless, noble form of truth-telling, or parrhesia: "Parrhesia is the courage of truth in the person who speaks and who, regardless of everything, takes the risk of telling the whole truth that he thinks, but it is also the interlocutor's courage in agreeing to accept the hurtful truths that he hears."[3] In the classical paradigms he takes as his case studies, this takes the form of a heroic confrontation between nobles. For the speaker to be heard, he must have standing, he must be trusted, and he should be speaking against his own interests and at risk to himself (thereby banishing the suspicion that what he says is motivated by self-interest). The speaker's information should be useful, important; it should not stir up controversy for controversy's sake—the speaking of this truth should have a socially productive purpose. The sovereign before whom this speaker appears must be willing to absorb and integrate the speaker's difficult news.

The forms of alethurgy through which power expresses itself depend on a system that secures the place of speaker and listener and the value of what is said and heard. These rituals and procedures reveal truths a community needs to know in order to hold its shape—other forms of truth sink into alethurgy's shadows. These truths are whispered. They are held by an elder's silence, a mother's hysteria, a friend's addiction.

The women encountered in the Euripidean tragedies that organize Foucault's thoughts speak from these dark places. Because they are women, their truth-telling cannot take the heroic form even as their truths often generate the narrative's conditions of possibility. Take the contrast between title character of *Ion* and his noblewoman mother Creusa. Creusa was raped by Apollo. Ion is the fruit of that assault; she abandons her infant and assumes he was devoured by vultures. Ion grows up unaware of his noble blood; she is unaware of his fate. For a good portion of the drama, Creusa and Ion orbit each other without knowing that they are mother and son. Ion's struggle centers in his desire to occupy a position of power and authority within the courts: the fact that he was a foundling stands in the way of his ambition. The revelation of Creusa's truth will bestow on Ion the noble status he needs.[4] Creusa's grievance takes a different form. There is no king to whom she can present her case. Apollo never makes an appearance in this play, and so where Ion gets to plead his case before Power, the dramatic monologue in which Creusa indicts Apollo as her rapist is chanted, basically, to her father's elderly tutor—a slave ("How, o my soul, shall I be silent, how / Disclose this secret? Can I bid farewell / To modesty? What else restrains my tongue?" "Will I conceal this bed, but ease my breast, / The oppressive load discharged. Mine eyes drop tears, / My soul is rent, to wretchedness ensnared / By men, by gods, whom I will now disclose, / Unkind betrayers of the beds they forced").[5]

Foucault observes that, in the drama, the moving speech in which Creusa presents her truth—that she was raped by Apollo—"is what we could call an instance of personal (as opposed to political) *parrhesia*."[6] When Ion speaks his truth, his "*parrhesia* takes the form of truthful political criticism. Creusa's *parrhesia*," in contrast, "takes the form of a truthful accusation against another more powerful than she, and as a confession of the truth about herself."[7] Ion critiques a system that denies him. Creusa's critique is immanent to, embedded within, the avowal of her violation. Creusa's discourse is an accusation made against a god who raped her and never appears before her again. The outrage that she expresses has nowhere to go. And yet that personal truth amplifies and credentializes Ion's capacities as a truth-teller; her truth births the ironies of Ion's situation. I am tempted to say that her truth is the site of drama; her son's is the site of politics.

Foucault steers clear of Cassandra's mesmerizing appearances in *The Trojan Women* and in Aeschylus's *Agamemnon*. Cassandra is the figure to whom most of us who think about these things turn. At the latter drama's opening, Cassandra is wheeled onstage in the king's chariot; she is a war trophy and sex slave. Another of Apollo's victims, Cassandra is gifted with prophesy and, infamously, doomed to never be believed (according to some versions of this myth, she is cursed for refusing his attempts to seduce her). In this play she stands silent for a very long stretch and then, left alone onstage with the chorus, she releases an unintelligible wail that organizes itself into Apollo's name ("OTOTOI POPOI DA! Apollo! O!pollo! Woepollo! O!").[8] From there, she maps out the drama's future disaster in a disturbed chant that no one onstage understands. The audience gets it, of course: she forecasts Agamemnon's death at the hands of his wife, and her own murder ("I'm just a killed slave, easy fistful of death").[9]

Cassandra, at once a beloved and repulsive figure in feminist thought, represents the burden of witnessing. These kinds of characters (usually, in classical drama, slaves, women, and exiles) are present for the abandonment of babies in the wild; they see the relevant murder with their own eyes and know where the bodies are buried.[10] Because the truths they carry seem to float off their bodies, this figure must be squirreled away until the alethurgic machine requires her presence to resolve the drama's central conflicts. Where the heroic forms of parrhesia explored by Foucault unfold within a structure that allows the testing of different aspects of parrhesiatic discourse (e.g., the speaker's credibility, the value of what they say), one can't test Cassandra's discourse for truth—her truth is out of time. Because she articulates the disaster of the future, her discourse has the disorienting truth of a curse.

Cassandra thus does not figure the courage of "fearless speech"—quite the opposite. Before she leaves the stage, for example, Clytemnestra tries and fails to engage the captive: "I'm talking to you, Kassandra," she says. "Oh she's mad. . . . Brought from a captured city yet she knows not how to take the bit—she frets her inside mouth away in foam of blood."[11] In her survey of dramaturgical approaches to *Agamemnon*, Yopie Prins observes that Cassandra appears as "less a speaking character defined by action than a written character that enacts the strangeness of its own speaking." She "seems destroyed by her own utterance."[12] In this sense, she is a paradigmatic figure for the rape victim who speaks of her own violation, and who, furthermore, embodies the larger crisis of which her rape is a mere example. "Cassandra," writes Anne Carson, in the introduction to her translation of the play, "is a self-consuming truth."[13] She is, in and of herself, the manifestation of a truth about power. Cassandra was once a remote figure; today, Rebecca Solnit writes in "Cassandra among the Creeps," she has moved into the mainstream. On some days, this form of truth-teller is an instrument of justice; on others, she is a craven snitch.

The discourse of harassment—the language of the victim and the abuser—slides back and forth across the lines that divide and connect speakable and unspeakable forms of truth. Rape culture, one must point out, does not just make sexual violence more possible. It patterns the whole of our thinking about sex, race, gender, and sexuality—for if it makes rape more possible, it also makes rape feel unknowable, unavoidable, beyond narration and account. And so, for some of us, when we are raped, we can't use the word, because what happened might have been awful, but was it *that* awful? We are cornered by rape's singularity and its ubiquity.

Rape culture alibis harassment; it materializes as authority and entitlement. It names some forms of sexual violence rape and others ritual. It mobilizes a sense of sexual security behind a culture of incarceration. It created the sex offender and throws him into a black hole as a way of disavowing the banality of sexual coercion. Rape culture thrives in the gaslight, casting trans people as monstrous shadows invading feminine space. It cements *woman* to *rape*, spinning out crazy narratives of biology and destiny—it wraps its arms around the idea of man and woman, biological sex, and puts trans women into a horrifying chokehold.

The relationship between sex, violence, knowledge, and truth is a defining preoccupation of feminist critical theory. It is, in many ways, the foundation of feminist literary criticism: "epistemic violence," for example, is a key term in Gayatri Spivak's "Can the Subaltern Speak?"; the project of thinking about the relationship between race, sex, knowledge, and power is the defining preoccupation of Patricia Hill Collins's *Black Feminist Thought*. Eve Kosofsky Sedgwick's *Epistemology of the Closet* interrogates knowledge/ignorance dynamics as they unfold around sex: "The epistemological asymmetry," she writes, "of the laws that govern rape, privileges at the same time men and ignorance, inasmuch as it matters not at all what the raped woman perceives just as long as the man raping her can claim not to have noticed (ignorance in which male sexuality receives careful education)."[14] Barbara Johnson writes, "There are two things women are silent about: their pleasure and their violation. The work performed by [the] idealization of this silence . . . helps culture not be able to tell the difference between the two."[15] Johnson points to the title of Katie Roiphe's 1993 antifeminist best seller, *The Morning After: Sex, Fear, and Feminism on Campus*, which "implicitly ties that undecidability not to a silence that does cultural work but to the question of retrospective individual interpretation ('one person's rape is another person's bad night')."[16] Roiphe's book adopts its own truth-telling posture; in her case, she presents herself as speaking a truth that women, in a feminist context, are supposed to keep to themselves—in this narrative, women do not know what they want and feel a pressure from other women to cry rape. One can say something similar of Laura Kipnis's *Unwanted Advances*, published nearly twenty-five years later. A chapter titled "Flip Flopping on Consent" opens with the following warning: "Sexual consent can now be retroactively withdrawn (with official sanction) years later, based on changing feelings or residual ambivalence, or new circumstances. Please note that this makes anyone who's ever had sex a potential rapist."[17] In this discursive environment, sexual pleasure and violation coemerge within a theater of confusion; every rumor feels true and yet every accusation feels false, and that is, for those who are into this narrative, what makes sex sexy. Here, we encounter the lenticular shimmer of the skeptical discourse that makes the difference between abuser and abused into a matter of perspective alone, and that is rape culture's truth.

Sharon Marcus, in her widely cited 1992 essay "Fighting Bodies, Fighting Words: A Theory and Politics of Rape Prevention," addresses the debilitating character of much discourse on rape. Rape culture normalizes the positioning of women as objects of violence rather than as agentic subjects within violence. It furthermore situates sexual violation as an absolute trauma: in rape culture, rape is the worst. Rape culture is distinguished by both skepticism and pessimism: if women can't be believed, they are also destined for the worst. Sexual violation, within rape culture—and its cousin "Law and Order" feminism—is taken to be a fundamental, defining aspect of women's being and an expression of women's place within an organic distribution of power (and so criminal law is articulated around a normalization of white women's sexual vulnerability and an expansion of the sense of social threat posed by the sex offender). This liberal feminist discourse can "produce a sense of futility: rape seems to be taken for granted as an occurrence and only postrape events offer possible occasions for intervention."[18] It can reify rape "as terrifyingly unnameable and unrepresentable, a reality that lies beyond our grasp and which we only experience as grasping and encircling us."[19] This line of thinking, Marcus continues, "often concurs with masculinist culture in its designation of rape as a fate worse than or tantamount to death; the apocalyptic tone which it adopts and the metaphysical status which it assigns to rape implies that rape can only be feared or legally repaired, not fought."[20] (Cassandra speaks from that dead zone.)

Skeptics like Roiphe and Kipnis tend to universalize these expressions of masculinist power; abuse dynamics are folded into a sense of sex as an expression of inherent power differentials. Power, in this view, is, in and of itself, sexy. Victims, in these narratives, suffer from their own naivete and/or from confusion about the nature of their real desire. These narratives, furthermore, tend to lean on legal discourses about rape as if its structures and requirements were the best tools available with which we can account for sexual abuse and harassment. The importance of the phrase "beyond a reasonable doubt," specific to the requirements for findings of guilt within a criminal court system in the United States, is expanded within skeptical discourse to authorize the decredentialization of the victim's narrative in social and professional contexts. One should, in general, be suspicious of people who mobilize the language of the criminal court system to legitimize their positions vis-à-vis sexual violence: at minimum it betrays an identification with patriarchal and racist structures of power. I return here to Foucault's observation of the relationship between power and alethurgy—state-authorized truth-telling rituals work to reproduce and consolidate the structures of power. The transformation of those structures is initiated by other rituals, other forms of truth. The criminal justice system's failure of victims of sexual violence is so pervasive, so complete and total, that the project of abolishing the criminal justice system and all of its institutions is led, in fact, by feminists of color attempting to address the problem of intimate partner violence within their communities.[21]

Marcus theorizes rape as an articulation of power, as an iteration of "conventional, gendered structures of feeling and action." Its grammar shapes our sense of the possible and is written into the body: "The language of rape speaks through us," she writes, "freezing our own sense of force and affecting the would-be rapist's perceptions of our lack of strength."[22] We should think of the dominant discourse of rape as a specific organization of the relationship of sex, violence, gender, and truth. Rape appears in this discursive world as the Real—it grounds a language of violence and draws language's limits. This sense of rape is a defining element in the pessimism that clings to heterosexist and white supremacist thinking: a sense of gender difference is rooted in an absolute, unchangeable vulnerability expressing racial privilege and enabling racialized violence. The discourse of rape isolates rape from a continuum of violence, claims sex for itself (to redistribute), and forces the rape-able into an ontological and epistemological corner. Within the discourse of rape, rape is your truth in a way that the telling of it never can be. This whirlpool distorts our thinking about everything touched by the discourse of rape—it exerts a definitional force on our experiences of sexual harassment and our sense of sexual happiness, intimacy, and truth. And so some of us hold experiences of violation close, withholding the physical memory of violation from language with the hope that in doing so we will avoid being sucked into rape culture's engine.

Elena Ferrante's *Neapolitan* novels account for truths you will not find in case literature and invite us to reflect on how we receive stories about suffering as a sexual subject. Gender-based forms of violence are so seamlessly integrated into the violent landscape of her work, so soaked into her exploration of what it means to be to poor, it is easy to miss their importance. As Tiziana de Rogatis explains, sexual violence is part of a "labyrinth of violence" that shapes, corners, and traps Ferrante's characters.[23] As is true of so much feminist literature, there is no question if Ferrante's characters are raped. The novels' dramatic intensities are not generated by melodramas of uncertainty about any character's violation. The discourse of rape nevertheless structures the narrator's sense of sex and knowledge, her experience of her own violation, and the friendship at the heart of the *Neapolitan* project.

The narrator of the *Neapolitan* quartet is a writer named Elena Greco; the subject of these novels is her relationship to her friend Lila. Like Ferrante, Elena Greco's reputation is defined by how she writes about women's lives. She is in her sixties by the time we meet her, and while she has enjoyed many years as a widely respected author, her work has fallen out of fashion. At the height of her career, however, public debate about literature and sexual politics was oriented by the question of where one stood regarding a scandalous sex scene in her quasi-autobiographical novel. As Ferrante's narrator moves into a public life, at nearly every reading she is asked to explain why she "had considered it necessary to write, in such a polished story, a risqué part."[24] Over the course of the series, we learn that the scandalous sexual adventure she writes into her novel is based on her personal experience. But where, in that novel, the narrator has casual public sex with an older friend of the family, in the text that we read, the narrator has casual public sex with an older friend of the family who, a couple years earlier, molested her. The narrator of Ferrante's novel confesses that this (the novel we read) is, in fact, the first time she has told that story. She never discusses this incident with Lila, her closest friend; she makes this disclosure only after Lila disappears and Elena commits to writing down "all the details of [their] story, everything that still remained in [her] memory."[25]

My Brilliant Friend (the first in the series) tracks the divergence of Elena and Lila's paths as the former advances into middle school and the latter is pushed out of it by her violent family. The entire series is animated with a sense of Lila's capacity. She is clever, mischievous, resistant, creative, spontaneous. Elena longs for Lila to find her interesting. They read *Little Women* together, and Lila suggests they write a book themselves. Elena is thrilled, but busy, and puts Lila off. Lila sits down and writes a story herself. At this point, they are elementary school children. Elena is so enamored with the beauty of Lila's story, "The Blue Fairy," that she shows it to her teacher. Maestra Oliviero, aware that Lila is withdrawing from school, brushes the story aside and tells Elena to focus on her own work: "If one wishes to remain a plebian, he, his children, the children of his children deserve nothing. Forget Cerullo [Lila] and think only of yourself" (*MBF*, 72).

Lila is beaten by her father and by her brother across much of the first novel ("every time Lila and I met I saw a new bruise" [*MBF*, 204]). Constrained by her family's refusal to support her schooling, Lila's life possibilities narrow quickly. She begins to sour, and the narrator defends herself against the pull of Lila's misery by carving out "secret pathways into a need of my own to be superior" (*MBF*, 81). She rubs Lila's face in her "better report card" and in the fact that Elena "would go to middle school and [Lila] would not" (*MBF*, 81). At the moment their childhood path splits, just as Elena graduates and moves up and Lila is exiled from the classroom, the narrator swings by her friend's house and, from the street, hears Lila arguing with her father: "Suddenly, the shouting stopped and a few seconds later my friend flew out the window, passed over my head, and landed on the asphalt behind me" (*MBF*, 82). Lila is lucky; only her arm is broken.

When I first read that sentence, I knew I had to write about what Larry Nassar's patients had been through—I saw them flying, tumbling. Twisting joints, breaking bones, and landing on his table. A parade of injuries. I thought about the girls and young women who tried to talk about what he was doing, and who were shunned by their teammates and coaches; I thought about the ones who complained and then returned to their team and to his table. I thought about the way one feels lucky relative to other victims—creeping backward from them, lest you be sucked in by the undertow that sweeps them away.

As the narrator applies herself to her studies, Lila begins to experience the world as saturated by histories of violence, inequity, and exploitation. She becomes a teen angel of history who leads her friends on grim tours of their neighborhood, pointing to one house in which someone was tortured and to the stones across which fascists marched. For Lila, "there are no gestures, words, or sighs that do not contain the sum of all the crimes that human beings have committed and commit" (*MBF*, 154). She is gripped by a "frenzy of absolute disclosure" (*MBF*, 154). While Lila is electrified by the unveiling of the history of violence that saturates her neighborhood, she is also in the process of being subdued by it. She marries one man to escape the unwanted advances of another who stalks and threatens her ("He's been obsessed with me for a long time, and even runs after the shadow of my shadow").[26] At the start of the next book in the series (*The Story of a New Name*), we learn that Lila is violently raped by her new husband on their honeymoon. That husband, Ferrante writes, needed to pass on the lesson that he had been taught: "Your wife has to learn right away that she is female and you're the male and she has to obey."[27] Lila refuses this lesson, and so the rape is brutal. "What are you doing?" her new husband yells at her as he holds her down; "Be quiet. You're just a twig and if I want to break you I will break you." He bites, slaps, and hits her until she understands that "if she continued to resist he would certainly kill her." And so, Ferrante writes, "Lila emptied herself of all rebellion, yielding to a wordless terror" (*TSNN*, 42). The narrator continues, "When, after some awkward attempts, he tore her flesh with passionate brutality, Lila was absent" (*TSNN*, 42).

The story of Lila's rape is recorded in her personal notebooks; Lila gives these to the narrator because she is afraid her husband might find them. Elena is mesmerized and troubled by Lila's words: "The notebooks exuded the force of seduction that Lila had given off since she was a child" (*TSNN*, 16). After she reads them, she drops the journals into the Arno River: "I couldn't stand feeling Lila on me and in me. . . . I placed the box on the parapet, and pushed it slowly, a little at a time, until it fell into the river, as if it were her, Lila in person, plummeting, with her thoughts, words, the malice with which she struck back at anyone, the way she appropriated me, as she did every person or thing or event or thought that touched her: books and shoes, sweetness and violence, the marriage and the wedding night" (*TSNN*, 18). It is a strange response to her friend's writing, especially given that Elena has a story of her own.

Elena is molested on the night of her fifteenth birthday while working as a caretaker for a family vacationing at a beachside town. Elena is in love with Nino Sarratore, whose family is staying at the same house; Nino, however, is not in love with her. Amplifying her sense of rejection, although she writes regularly to Lila all summer, Lila does not respond until Elena threatens to stop sending letters. Sensing her loneliness, Nino's father, Donato, gives her attention.

In the week leading up to her birthday, Donato's easy, affable company takes the sting out of Elena's loneliness. Donato, a conductor, poet, and journalist, has a reputation in the neighborhood; he seduced a widow and then dropped her, abandoning her to madness.

Donato is good at making Elena feel special. His attentions, however, mean little when compared with the transformative effect of the one letter that Lila sends. That letter captivates Elena: "The voice set in the writing overwhelmed me, enthralled me even more than when we talked face to face: it was completely cleansed of the dross of speech" (*MBF*, 227). She spends the day after she receives it, her birthday, trying and failing to write a letter that matches her friend's brilliance. She is so moved by Lila's narration of her troubles and so certain of the poverty of her own writing that she tells the family for which she's working that she will leave early, to tend to her friend in person. On the night of her birthday, she takes "the most precious things [she] owned" (*MBF*, 231) to bed with her: a bookmark of Nino's and Lila's letter ("I kissed the bookmark as I did every night, I tried to reread my friend's letter in the weak glow" [*MBF*, 231]). The sexualization of reading/writing is not subtle: Nino's bookmark manages the narrator's relationship, as a reader, to Lila's writing.

Donato enters the kitchen in which Elena sleeps and sits on the bed. He tells her, "Don't think about your friend" (*MBF*, 232), much as Elena had been told by her teacher, "Forget Cerullo."

He pushed the sheet aside, continuing to kiss me with care, with passion, and he sought my breast with his hand, he caressed me under the nightgown. Then he let go, descended between my legs, pressed two fingers hard over my underpants. I said, did nothing, I was terrified by that behavior, by the horror it created, by the pleasure that I nevertheless felt. I didn't move, I don't know for how long. However I tried to distance the sensation of his tongue, his caresses, the pressure of his hand I couldn't. . . . I felt an uncontainable hatred for Donato Sarratore and disgust for myself, for the pleasure that lingered in my body. . . . I remained in the same position for many hours. Then, at first light, I shook myself, collected all of my things, took apart the bed, wrote two lines of thanks to Nella, and left. (*MBF*, 232)

This passage concludes with the revelation that this is, for the narrator, a series of disclosures: "However unlikely it may seem today, as long as I could remember until that night I had never given myself pleasure, I didn't know about it, to feel it surprised me" (*MBF*, 232). Furthermore, until she writes the book that we are reading, she had never "sought words for that unexpected end to my vacation" (*MBF*, 233).

In the following novel (*The Story of a New Name*, which opens with the story of Lila's rape), Elena Greco runs into Donato on the beach. At seventeen, Elena is still in love with Nino. She is again spending her summer helping a family with their kids. Elena encourages Lila to visit her, in part because she knows it will make her more interesting to Nino, whom she adores; she knows that he is attracted to Lila. Things go badly; Lila and Nino have an affair. Cementing this triangulation, Lila enlists Elena as the alibi who allows them to have sex. In the very moment she is performing this service for her friend, Elena goes for a walk on the beach and gives in to her sense of abandonment.

I hope that from this darkness packs of mad dogs will emerge, vipers, scorpions, enormous sea serpents. I hope that while I'm sitting here, on the edge of the sea, assassins will arrive out of the night and torture my body. Yes, yes, let me be punished for my insufficiency, let the worst happen, something so devastating that it will prevent me from facing tonight, tomorrow, the hours and days to come, reminding me with always more crushing evidence of my unsuitable constitution. . . . Then someone said, "Lena," and touched my shoulder with cold fingers. I started, an icy grip seized my heart and when I turned suddenly and recognized Donato Sarratore, the breath burst in my throat like the sip of a magic potion, the kind that in poems revives strength and the urge to live. (*TSNN*, 289–90)

When she has sex with Donato, Elena Greco explicitly positions her decision against the background noise of the molestation. "The entire time," she tells us, "I didn't once regret having accepted what was happening. I had no second thoughts and I was proud of myself, I wanted it to be like that" (*TSNN*, 291). To make it absolutely clear that she is inscribing herself as an agent into the discourse of rape, she tells us, "I imposed it on myself" (*TSNN*, 291). The melodramatic intensity, the Gothic convulsions of this passage urge us to see this sexual adventure within a larger, crisis-ridden story of attachment and abandonment. Later, her memories of that night inform her feelings about her fiancé, Pietro, and other lovers from her past.

Discussion of the "risqué parts" of Ferrante's writing rarely reconcile the narrator's molestation by Donato with her later decision to lose her virginity to him.[28] In *Unwanted Advances*, Laura Kipnis imagines that today's students, "schooled in the simplistic catechisms of the moment" and not up to the "complicated business" (48) of sexuality, are not capable of absorbing the "ferocious emotional complexity" (49) of work like Ferrante's. By way of example, Kipnis points to the scene on the beach:

Elena decides to lose her virginity to Donato Sarratore, the father of the boy she's in love with. She's sixteen or seventeen at the time, and on the one hand, Donato disgusts her — his flowery language ("sleazy lyricizing"), his advanced age. Yet she's weirdly sexually compelled by him. She likes how he makes her feel. She wants to feel like a different person: he's her transit to a new self. After they have sex she reflects that she has no regrets, then coldly dumps him. Later she'll look back on the episode with more mixed feelings, but in the moment, it feels empowering.[29]

She makes no mention of the fact that he had molested Elena. Christina Lupton describes Sarratore as "a man who desires and arouses [Elena], but for whom, there is never any question, she feels no love."[30] Like Kipnis, Lupton suggests a contradiction between the sexual politics of Ferrante's novel and the emerging zeitgeist, on the cusp of #metoo. Lupton asks, "What did it mean that liberal intellectuals in this moment celebrated a work of fiction whose core scene [meaning, that scene on the beach] depicts acts for which this same audience would want to prosecute a real Donato?" Neither critic fully articulates the reason that Elena's decision might challenge readers. Both draw from popular discourse collapsing antirape activism with a certain kind of liberal feminist reader—a woman who is easily offended, whose sexual pleasures betray her sexual politics, a woman whose primary understanding of sexual transgression is articulated in relation to the law.

Kipnis discusses Ferrante's novel for only one paragraph on her way to declaring a desire to test student limits: "As a teacher," Kipnis explains, "I do what I can to get [students] to think about their responses to the world as questions, not givens; to forestall the easy moralizing. When I really want to cause my supposedly sexually with-it students a world of despair, I like to bring up Freud. 'If we didn't desire to have sex with our parents, why would we need to have a taboo?'"[31] She lingers over the point, positioning herself as a maverick who pushes students to confront their naive selves. Discomfort, unease, even humiliation are taken for granted here as signs that a student is learning. Student reticence is read as prudishness, inexperience as failure. This pedagogical posture has a broad appeal; one finds it in think pieces, in op-eds, and in hallway conversations among faculty aggrieved by their students' discomfort with sexually frank material.

As a close reader drawn to representations of sexual life and as a teacher committed to bringing that material into the classroom, I want to pause here to say that one should not take student unease about the sexually frank material they encounter in the classroom as an indication of what students know/ don't know or are/are not comfortable with in their lives outside that classroom. Students who seem comfortable with talking about such material in class are not necessarily at ease with sexuality—they might be anxious about appearing uncomfortable and compensate by showing off their sophistication to the teacher and to the other students. (Elena, in fact, spends no small amount of time pretending to just this sort of sophistication.) It is also worth remembering that the incest taboo that Kipnis uses to tease her students does not only manage children's attachments to parents. What does it mean, for instance, to rhetorically position your adult students as children in a pedagogical exercise designed to expose their unspeakable desires? When we bring sex into the classroom as a subject of conversation, we bring not only our students' desires into a space of reflection—we bring our own, and students see this. If, as a teacher, you enjoy teasing students with their disavowed desire for their parents, you might be projecting onto those students a desire for them to desire you, as you imagine they really desire their parents. What is a good student supposed to do, exactly, when you have placed them in that position? The vulnerabilities of sexual life are cemented into the humiliations of the classroom: the only acceptable, habitable posture for the good student in that scenario is that of one who has mastered the reading—professor and student exchange jokes, snide chuckles, knowing giggles. Those who don't play along must have something wrong with them. That dynamic is not incidental to the sexual politics of Ferrante's writing or, frankly, Nassar's grooming tactics (victims describe Nassar as "goofy" and as constantly making sexual jokes during treatment).

Bringing sex talk into your work is difficult: doing so has all sorts of effects, some of which can be empowering, some of which can be disabling. When Elena draws her experiences with Donato into her first novel, it gets away from her. Elena Greco's book has a bad reputation. Her brothers defend Elena against neighbors who call her a whore. Her mother demands to know if she wrote about "the disgusting things [she] goes around doing."[32] A friend describes her as "brave" for writing about "the things [she] do[es] on the beach" (*TOWL*, 90); Elena disowns that writing by claiming that it is the character who does it, not she, but we know that is a lie. Men take her writing as an invitation. An older friend of her publisher chaperones her on a book tour and tells her that the dirty parts of her book are not really that dirty. He recommends that she read Henry Miller, and then he makes an unwanted advance in an elevator (*TOWL*, 66). Not long after this, Elena experiences a more disturbing encounter with a reader she meets at a party. The group, a bohemian set of activists, discusses her book and dismisses it as having no political value. Later, one of the guests sneaks into the room where she is sleeping. Taking Donato's place, Juan sits on at the foot of her bed:

> "You're a writer, you write about love. Everything that happens to us feeds the imagination and helps us to create. Let me be near you, it's something you'll be able to write about."
>
> He touched my foot with the tips of his fingers. I couldn't bear it. I leaped up and turned on the light.
>
> "Out," I hissed and in such a peremptory tone, so clearly close to shouting, so determined to attack and to fight with all my energy, that he got up, slowly, and said with disgust:
>
> "You're a hypocrite." (*TOWL*, 82)

Stunned by this episode, she returns to the scene of her abuse: "Suddenly I thought of what had happened with Donato Sarratore. Not so much the evening on the beach in Ischia, which I had transformed into the episode in the novel, but the time he appeared in Nella's kitchen, when I had just gone to bed, and he had kissed me, touched me, causing a flow of pleasure against my very will" (*TOWL*, 83). "What did I display?" the narrator asks. "Between the girl of then, astonished, frightened, and the woman attacked in the elevator, the woman who had been subjected to that incursion now, was there a connection?" (*TOWL*, 83). That question carries a particular resonance for conversations about sexual harassment. Forms of sexual subjection accumulate and amplify each other.

In the last novel in the series, years into their relationship, Elena stumbles on Nino having sex with their housekeeper over the bathroom sink. She catches his eye in the mirror. Nino's expression, Ferrante writes, "was the expression of his father, Donato, not when he deflowered [Elena] on the Maronti but when he touched [her] between the legs, under the sheet, in Nella's kitchen" (*TSLC*, 239). More disturbing is what Elena sees in Sylvana, "a woman who cleaned my house, did my shopping, cooked, took care of my children; a woman marked by the struggle to survive, large, worn-out, the absolute opposite of the cultivated, elegant women [Nino] brought to dinner" (*TSLC*, 238–39). Sylvana is, in other words, an adult version of child-Elena (who was working as a mother's helper when Donato molested her), a mirror image of adult-Lila (who loses her seductiveness under the grind of factory work). Sylvana is any woman at work; she is the woman Elena is terrified of becoming.

The banalization of sexual violation in Ferrante's novels contrasts sharply with one of Ferrante's literary touchstones, Elsa Morante's 1974 novel *La Storia* (*History: A Novel*), which examines the lives of a poor Roman family living through World War II. That Zola-like novel opens with nearly one hundred pages of writing offering the story of a rape: a German soldier looking for company stumbles on an Italian woman whom he coerces into inviting into her home, and then assaults. Neither speaks the other's language. The rape has two stages: the soldier penetrates Ida in a physically violent assault, and then has sex with her again, in a manner intended to draw her pleasure from her. The story of the rape is complicated by the fact that Ida is epileptic; she has a seizure during the first assault (and so has no memory of it beyond that it happened) and experiences the second during that seizure's postictal phase—her memory of that assault is watery and fantastical.[33] As Morante moves between the soldier's perspective and Ida's, the reader learns that their inability to understand each other is a crucial condition of possibility for the rape: Ida, who has been keeping her Jewish heritage a secret, is rightly scared of the soldier and experiences his attempts at seduction through absolute terror. She allows him into her apartment because she does not feel as if she has any choice. Gunther has no awareness of what his uniform means to her, and so her responses to him confuse and then frustrate him. The disaster of their encounter is escalated by her seizure: she cries out *No* as she feels the seizure coming on. As if activated by a primitive mechanism, he rapes her in response to that *No*. Afterward, he fixes a lamp in her apartment and "exchanges" mementos with Ida—he leaves her his treasured pocketknife and takes a fading flower from a bouquet on the table. As Lydia Oram writes in her analysis of these passages, he is a "paradoxically innocent assailant" who experiences his own violence within the script of "any normal adolescent amorous exchange."[34] He dies in the war a few days later; she, however, spends the rest of her life marked by the shame of the experience and by the fear that he could return. History is written onto Ida's body by that rape, and one can read in that rape the whole history of World War II Italy. Sexual violence is important to Ferrante's *Neapolitan* novels, but it is decidedly not epic. This is what grabs us.

The difference in how sex matters in these four novels reflects Ferrante's focus: Elena and Lila's friendship is the primary focus of the *Neapolitan* novels. Their experiences of sexual violation matter because their friendship is shaped by them. That these novels are centered in the grief structure of heterosexual friendships between women could not be more explicit: Elena Greco only begins to write these novels after Lila disappears, taking with her every material trace of her sixty-six years of existence. Ferrante's novels return us to the stories of lost possibility that drove so much queer theory in the early 1990s: heterosexual gender identity positions, Judith Butler argued in *Gender Trouble*, can be understood as haunted by the melancholic incorporation of lost love possibilities—meaning, by the grief and loss initiated especially by homophobic prohibitions against attachments to members of the same sex.[35]

In what she describes as a "queer counterfactual" reading of the novels, Jill Richards aligns the moment Elena slides Lila's writing into the Arno River with the "queer love plot that might have been."[36] Richards is one of the few critics to take note of just how close Elena comes to making the desire for her friend explicit. Not unlike Jo March, who, in her struggle with her feelings about the loss of her sister Meg to a marriage proposal, asks, "Why can't I just marry Meg myself?," Elena, as she witnesses Lila's wedding, daydreams about running away with Lila.[37] In this fantasy, she and Lila "go and live far away, lightheartedly descending together all the steps of humiliation, alone, in unknown cities" (*TSNN*, 119). This is a charming if weak resolution to the challenge of the narrator's attachment to her friend. It is overshadowed by a different set of fantasies, more explicitly structured by the forms of sexual violence that organize both characters' lives.

On the morning of Lila's wedding, Elena is nearly overcome by desire as she gives her friend a bath:

> I had never seen her naked, I was embarrassed. Today I can say that it was the embarrassment of gazing with pleasure at her body, of being the not impartial witness of her sixteen-year-old's beauty a few hours before Stefano touched her, penetrated her, disfigured her, perhaps, by making her pregnant. At the time it was just a tumultuous sensation of necessary awkwardness, a state in which you cannot avert your gaze or take away the hand without recognizing your own turmoil, without, by that retreat, declaring it, hence without coming into conflict with the undisturbed innocence of the one who is the cause of the turmoil, without expressing by that rejection the violent emotion that overwhelms you, so that it forces you to stay, to rest your gaze on the childish shoulders, on the breasts and stiffly cold nipples, on the narrow hips and tense buttocks, on the black sex, on the long legs, on the tender knees, on the curved ankles, on the elegant feet: and to act as if it's nothing, when instead everything is there, present, in the poor dim room, amid the worn furniture, on the uneven, water-stained floor, and your heart is agitated, your veins inflamed. (*MBF*, 312–13)

As Richards observes, critical discussion of sex, intimacy, and love in these novels tends to locate friendship in the story of Elena and Lila, and sex in the story of their relationships with men.[38] This requires the suppression of these paragraphs and a broad minimization of the importance of the narrator's attachment to Lila in shaping the work's ecology of desire—a remarkable elision given the anchoring of Ferrante's literary project in one woman's attachment to the other. Elena's fantasy is, at least in my reading, an echo and revision of her own experience of violation and not-knowing; Elena steps into Donato's place in relation to her friend's body and then goes on to insert herself into Lila's place and to insert them both into sexual geometries in which she and her friend are violated, alongside each other, by the men in their lives.

> I had a confusion of feelings and thoughts: embrace her, weep with her, kiss her, pull her hair, laugh, *pretend to sexual experience and instruct her in a learned voice, distancing her with words just at the moment of great-*

est closeness. But in the end there was only the hostile thought that I was washing her, from her hair to the soles of her feet, early in the morning, just so that Stefano could sully her in the course of the night. I imagined her naked as she was at that moment, entwined with her husband, in the bed in the new house, while the train clattered under their windows and his violent flesh entered her with a sharp blow, like the cork pushed by the palm into the neck of a wine bottle. And it suddenly seemed to me that the only remedy against the pain that I was feeling, that I would feel, was to find a corner secluded enough so that Antonio could do to me, at the same time, the exact same thing. (*MBF*, 313, emphasis added)

The conjunction of sexual ignorance/innocence, dispossession, and discovery that structures the scene in the kitchen shapes her relationship to Lila. If she can fantasize about "pretending to sexual experience" with her friend, it is because she has the experience of being subjected to another's performance of sexual knowledge over her own body. If she plays with the idea that she might use a pedagogical remove in order to amplify the fantasy's sexual intensity ("distancing [Lila] with words just at the moment of greatest closeness"), it might have something to do with Donato's intrusion into Elena's bedtime enjoyment of Lila's writing. He gives her the orgasm she doesn't dare to give herself; she imagines—but only imagines—doing the same to her friend and fantasizes that she denies her that orgasm by replacing the touch of her hand with words. That scenario is quickly subsumed by another fantasy in which Lila is violently penetrated by her new husband—a thought that gives Elena an exquisite pain which she embraces and resolves by taking Lila's place in this scenario. In the next novel, we learn that Elena acts on this fantasy of simultaneous violation—not in response to Lila's wedding, but in response to Lila's affair with Nino (one in which Lila violates Elena's trust). Elena elaborates on the erotic flows of a grammar of sex and power that aligns women's pleasure with dispossession and which, furthermore, triangulates women's desire for each other through that dispossession. Her assertion of an agentic position in desire is expressed in a fantasy staged around a girl's violation. We might think of this scenario as a gendery cousin to that described by Freud's essay "A Child Is Being Beaten." "My friend is being violated" articulates a scene of identification and enjoyment in which the subject of the fantasy (here, Elena, imagining Lila's "sullying") slides around the scene—Elena is in the room; she is Stefano, she is Lila, she is Donato, she is the scenario's author, their friendship is its setting.

This play with the relationship between innocence, sexual knowledge, and power recall the subject of Eve Kosofsky Sedgwick's essay "The Privilege of Unknowing: Diderot's *The Nun*" (which anticipates *Epistemology of the Closet*). In Sedgwick's reading of Denis Diderot's satirical and scandalous novel, forms of innocence and ignorance gather around explicit and yet un-named scenes of lesbian desire and women's sexual agency and orgasmic capacity. Diderot's text plays with a recognizable pornographic genre, the whore's dialogue, in which an older woman with an encyclopedic sexual knowledge transfers her wisdom to a younger woman. That younger woman might be a protégé in a brothel, a novice in a convent, or a bride learning from her mother. In *The Nun*, however, the storytelling position is occupied not by the wise woman but by the figure of the ingenue. She is a clean and impos-sibly blank slate who describes, in luscious detail, all that transpires around her as if she had no idea what was transpiring around her, for a reader who, in fact, always knows exactly what is going on. Diderot's narrator reports, for example, that while kissing her Mother Superior, "eventually a moment came, whether of pleasure or of pain I cannot say, when she went as pale as death, closed her eyes, and her whole body tautened violently, her lips were first pressed together and moistened with a sort of foam, then they parted and she seemed to expire with a deep sigh."[39] Sedgwick treats the "doggy, fascinated lingering at the very precisely unnamed threshold of delineation between 'the sexual' and the 'nonsexual'" as an intensely political scene.[40] The reader who does not recognize the intense eroticism of Diderot's text is, she observes, hard to imagine, and yet much in the novel's reception and much in the novel itself depends on just this fictive possibility. The rudest temptation of sexuality studies in literary criticism is this naming of the sex-ual—*See! It's all about sex!*—a declaration that lets us feel sophisticated in relation to the text, characters, readers, students.

Drawing from the dynamic relationship between power and ignorance in Diderot's text, Sedgwick urges readers to shift their understanding of politi-cal struggle away from an Enlightenment, liberal humanist model, in which that struggle is imagined as a fight against ignorance, in favor of the analysis of the mobilization and distribution of knowledge, ignorance, and innocence within power structures:

> If *ignorance* is not—as it evidently is not—a single Manichaean . . . maw of darkness from which the heroics of human cognition can occasionally wrestle facts, insights, freedoms, progress, perhaps there exists instead a

plethora of *ignorances*, and we may begin to ask questions about the labor, erotics, and economics of their human production and distribution. Insofar as ignorance is ignorance *of* a knowledge—a knowledge may itself, it goes without saying, be seen as either "true" or "false" under some other regime of truth—these ignorances, far from being pieces of the originary dark, are produced by and correspond to particular knowledges and circulate as particular regimes of truth.[41]

So very much discourse about sexual harassment continues to be staged at a remove from the insights of Sedgwick's work—harassment dynamics were central to the project of *Epistemology of the Closet*: her writing on Diderot, in fact, is repurposed in that book's introductory essay.

Snide think pieces about trigger warnings that mock people who ask for them, nostalgic longings for a time when one could hug a student or close the office door, defenses for the linguistic play that supposedly defines queer pedagogy reproduce the innocence/ignorance dynamic Sedgwick critiques, conjuring a vision of the student whose main problem is their ignorance and their desire to be parented—as if it wasn't, in fact, the finger-wagging professor conjuring this version of the student, over and over again.

Unexamined assumptions about power and sexual knowledge structure discourse like this. Privilege thrives on the forms of unlearning and unknowing that manage one's relationship to sexual violence and rests in the ability to project ignorance onto other bodies (which then become the objects of anger and abuse). For Sedgwick, these struggles with knowledge/ignorance dynamics begin with learning to read and with "knowing how to interpret signs of sexual meanings." "Both," she writes, "involve acrobatic leaps of yet unearned identification consolidated by yet more violent repudiation."[42] In our anxious movement along these paths, we are tempted (or bullied) into positioning ourselves as knowing more than at least *that* person. The pleasure of the reader's encounter with Diderot's narrator is an effect of the bottomless generosity with which she cedes this superior position vis-à-vis sexual knowledge (the reader always gets to feel more worldly than she). As she makes her case, Sedgwick pauses to offer the readers of her essay a different, lacerating rhetorical question: "Perhaps I appeal with a special confidence to the force of this energy in an audience for whom its inexhaustible renewal [the defense against a sense of not-knowing] is both a qualification and a professional deformation: if the energy of our fear of, loathing for, disidentification from, and at the same time fascination with the ignorance that is only barely not our own were to evaporate, what force on earth would drive the red pen through the papers?"[43]

We, as readers, might wonder at the fact that it is Lila who figures sexual innocence for Elena, given how often the narrator underlines Lila's uncanny capacity for insight, her sexual power, and the intensity of their attachment to each other. But, of course, we only sense Lila's knowledge/innocence through the haze of Elena's frustrated desire to have and to be, to lose and to find her friend. Neither Elena nor Lila resembles Diderot's impossibly naive narrator; the *Neapolitan* project is not satirical. But Elena and Lila's friendship is structured by the fantasies, the fear and loathing, the identification and disidentification that Sedgwick describes. Elena's narration of her molestation is written as an "ignorance that is only barely not [her] own." As she runs her hands over her friend's bony hips, Elena presents herself as not entirely unlike the figures that Diderot gathers around Suzanne, and who gather around Diderot's novel itself. She leans into a fantasy of her friend's "undisturbed innocence" and gives herself permission to pleasure in her own knowingness, as it is thrown into relief by the unknowing body she touches.

We should see Elena's knowing touch of her friend's unknowing body in relation to the myriad other instances in which Lila is presented in the narrator's story as a figure of sexual excess. After she loses her virginity to Donato, Elena compares the total absence of emotional fulfillment in herself to Lila's attachment to Nino, the nature of which she deduces while watching them part at the end of their tryst: "[Lila] was in a state without thoughts or images, as if in detaching herself from Nino she had forgotten in him everything of herself, even the capacity to say what had happened to her, what was happening. This difference between us made me sad" (*TSNN*, 294). This, we learn over time, is projection—she attributes a sexual abundance to Lila that Lila cannot live up to. Lila's interest in Nino is short lived (they have an affair, she leaves her husband, and they live together for twenty-three days). Across the novels, Lila shows less and less interest in sexual intimacy. In a long conversation in which Lila maps her struggles at a factory (where she and other women are sexually abused), she confesses to Elena that "fucking had never given her the pleasure she had expected as a girl" (*TOWL*, 174). In a series of disclosures, the difficulty of which "was set in the weariness in her face, in the trembling of her hands" (*TOWL*, 174), Lila explains that she did not like being penetrated, that she "had done everything that a man could want from a woman, and that even when she had wanted to conceive a child with Nino, and had become pregnant, the pleasure you were supposed to feel, particularly at that moment of great love, had been missing" (*TOWL*, 174).

Instead of talking with Lila about her own substantial experiences of sexual unhappiness, instead of making space to absorb what her friend was telling her, Elena withdraws into herself and meditates on something that Nino once told her: "[Lila's] really badly made: in her mind and in everything, even when it comes to sex" (*TOWL*, 36). She ruminates on what being so "badly made" means and then puts an end to the conversation that Lila tries to start. Elena tells a lie: "For me it's not like that" (*TOWL*, 174).

Faced with her friend's confession, Elena Greco says nothing about the time Donato molested her, nothing about the way men have behaved toward her, and nothing about the years of painful intercourse with her own husband. And she certainly does not advise her friend on how to give herself an orgasm—a lesson she once dreamed of offering. Elena sits across the table from her friend and tells not the truth of "me too" and "you too" but the lie, the disavowal and the wish of "not me."

My reading of Ferrante is meant to spotlight the importance of failures of reception—this is a long echo, an extension of my reading of the failed reception of Thomashow's complaint, and, truth be told, my own. It is a meditation on what patriarchy does to our relationships to women: on the fear and disgust that structures our relationship to victims and their stories.

Elena's sex writing is misread by men who take it to mean she is sexually available to them; where her writing occasions disclosures like Lila's, Elena stifles the flicker of recognition in herself; where she seeks Donato's company because he makes her feel important, he abuses that vulnerability to make himself feel important. When she catches Nino having sex with their maid, disgust with herself ricochets around the room and concentrates itself in a revulsion toward the maid's body. Ferrante's narrator invites us to see her "not me" as a deferral to the magnitude of Lila's suffering: her own experience seems so trivial by comparison with what her friend has endured ("What could I have told her that had any resemblance with what she was telling me?" [*TOWL*, 174]). She also explains that she and Lila are limited in what they can say to each other. The language available to them "was useful for attack and self-defense precisely because it was the language of violence, it hindered, rather than encouraged intimate confidences" (*TOWL*, 174). Her brilliant friend who never made it to middle school, however, found just the words to name, quite precisely, this important truth about her sexual life.

Ferrante leaves it to the reader to decide the character of Lila's lack of sexual fulfillment. It might be the residue of trauma—Lila is a survivor of child abuse, harassment, workplace abuse, physical assault, and rape. The novel is punishing of Lila: on top of everything else, her daughter is kidnapped and never seen again. Maybe the sexual life that could have made her happy is so far beyond the acceptable as to be, in the space of the novel, nearly unspeakable, if you can say such a thing about a thousand-page treatise on "my brilliant," flat-chested, tomboyish, angular, rebellious, want-to-be-Jo-March friend. But maybe, too, this novel is at least in part about the displacement work done by the stories we tell each other about what other women have been through, what other women want and don't want. These scenes chart the capacity of sexual violence—the social fact of it—to structure so many forms of intimacy, especially where and when that intimacy masquerades as, to quote Sedgwick again, "the killing pretense that a culture does not know what it knows."[44]

CONCLUSION

In search of a way to bring this to an end, I circle back to the moment I walked into my class to catch N announcing to my students that Eve Kosofsky Sedgwick had died. In my mind's eye, there is a mile between the back of the room, where I am standing, and the front, where I need to be. It would be nearly a year before I would learn that in N's experience, coded messages radiated out from me and held her fixed in my orbit. A few months later I would learn that two students were helping her by recording me. Then I learned that colleagues thought I sexualized the classroom, that my work was inappropriate and, because they'd listened to a secretly recorded video in which I'd told a student that I was fine, that I wasn't being harassed and stalked. More time passed before I learned that a colleague in my department had been telling people that I was the real stalker, that I'd harassed N and made the whole thing up. By then I was working with students who were themselves victims sifting through the wreckage of their own experiences, looking for the remains of their interests and fighting to recover their relationship to their work. Time passed, and I saw them move on. Some recovered their relationship to their work and finished their dissertations; others found themselves by walking away.

I have been slower to move on. As I finished this book, I was teaching the same course, in the same classroom. The room holds three hundred students. It has no windows. It feels like an old movie theater. The exits are in the back, behind the students. I do not often conjure the shooter scenario for myself, but in that room, it is hard not to.

From the start of term, I had trouble sleeping on the nights before my class. A hundred little worries crawled into my mind. In the minutes before the start of my lecture, I wrestled with the room's technology as if it was my enemy. I kept forgetting to start the app that allowed the course to be streamed and recorded. I struggled with the microphones we have to use; the sound system is terrible. The projectors and lighting are not set up for lecturing on visual art—to get a good look at images on the screens, you have to turn the lights in the room off. This means that, in that room, I lecture from the dark.

I started coming to the lecture hall the second the previous class was over—one day, I did this while students in that class were finishing up an exam. I was flustered to see that class running over its time. Not thinking at all of the students working on that exam, I walked down to the front of the room and started working on setting up my class. My lecture that day felt off; I could feel something was wrong. On my ride home, I realized that I'd been huffy, imperious. By the time I got home, the skin of my entitlement dropped away. *How dare that professor let that exam go so long!* turned into *What is wrong with me?* I opened my email account to apologize to that professor and saw a message from a student in her class. She wrote to tell me how callous I had been. Her language was professional, but that was the gist of the message. On my campus, it takes a lot for a student to reach out to a professor to tell them that they were wrong. A hot flash of shame washed over me.

It isn't like me to be precious about starting class on time. And it's not like me to forget what students are feeling when they are taking a test and run out of time. Running an exam in that room is awful, and taking an exam in that room is the worst. I know better than to fight that room's basic reality. I was struggling to assert control over the space. I felt trapped, suspicious of students, and angry.

I apologized to the students and the professor. I let myself start class late, worked on chilling out. I decided to stop teaching that course and to avoid working in that classroom. I need to let go, and I need to manifest that letting go in real, material ways.

When she spoke to the class about Eve's death, N meant no harm—quite the opposite. She did not lock me into that scene. That feeling of being trapped is not exactly about the stalking: it expresses a crisis in my relationship to students, and in my relationship to my job.

When I started to write about harassment, I reached for Eve's books. Her writings inform who I am here on this page. The nature of Eve's importance to me as her student, however, has always been hard to name. Our connection was pedagogical, which is to say that it was somewhere between work, friendship, and family. Eve had meaningful relationships with a number of her students. Some of those relationships grew into personal friendships that, over the years, made those people into chosen family. I would place myself near the edge of that inner circle.

When her archive became available to researchers, I went to North Carolina to explore the traces of her relationship to life, love, and work.[1] I followed that visit up with long, rewarding conversations with her husband, Hal.

Eve's archive is filled with postcards and valentines—most of them are handmade collages. I assume many are from Hal (not all are signed), but others are from friends and students. The structure of Eve's personal life made lots of room for us. Socially, the world around her did not feel organized by the relational cosmology that privileges romantic love, monogamous marriage, wealth acquisition, and reproduction. She and Hal married when they were quite young (she was nineteen, and still in college). For much of their marriage, however, they did not live together. Her relationship with Hal looked, to us, like a very special intimacy in a constellation of intimacies. She had us over to her house all the time—we'd celebrate people getting jobs, finishing their dissertations. But sometimes we watched TV, cooked for each other, worked at a craft table. She seemed to love her work and her life.

This blending of work and home was so much a part of who she was that when people memorialize her, they tend to quote the same sentence: "What I'm proudest of, I guess, is having a life where work and love are impossible to tell apart."[2] This line was inscribed on cards handed out at her memorial; it appears in obituaries and on the website for the archive of her papers.

People lean on these words when they think of Eve because we know from her writing that this is how she wanted to be remembered. The sentence appears early in *A Dialogue on Love*, a book-length prose poem tracing her conversations with her therapist:

> "The best thing," I'm telling Shannon one day, "I think the thing I
> most want somebody to know about how I've lived . . . Oh, I do seem
> to be confessing to you that I
>   have the secret vice

of mentally writing my
obituary!
Do you think you can bear it?"
Shannon mimes invitation.
"What I'm proudest of, I guess, is having a life where work and
love are impossible to tell apart."[3]

The ease of that sentence belies its difficulty. Consider the scene from which
this sentence emerges: a fantasy staged around a bashful display of pride, a
fantasy about our recollection of her, as we grieve her death. Part of me goes
with the story it tells—*Oh, yes, that's a good life!*—and another part of me
bristles at the idea of it. I don't believe it. Or perhaps I resent it: the life she
describes sounds like a luxury I can't afford. I turn the idea of the sentence
over in my head and ask myself, what am I resisting? What do I mean by
luxury and *afford*?

When I got to Durham, North Carolina, in the fall of 1991, Eve was recovering from her first treatment for breast cancer. Her community was anxious
about her health. Later that year, she learned that the treatment had been
successful. But, as she shares in *A Dialogue on Love*, after receiving a relatively good prognosis ("if the cancer ever does get me, it probably won't be
for years" [5]), an alien form of depression settled on her:

> And yet (I told him, settled in his office upstairs), it's not so clear to
> me that "depressed" is the right word for what I am. Depressed is
> what everyone says—
> I'm weeping in a lot of
> offices these days
> (and I'm sure the tears slipped over my lids as I said it). But I
> think I *know* depression. I have my own history of it; and it felt,
> twenty years ago when I was really subject to it, so much less
> bearable than this does. So much.
> "And yet you are crying now," Shannon says. (2–3)

While she worked on *Dialogue*, she expanded her creative practice. She made
felt sculptures, artist books, and fabric wall-pieces.

Her interests were already shifting when her cancer came back. Eve writes
about the forms of awareness that grew around this diagnosis in a late essay,
"Reality and Realization." There, she shares her experience of being sus-
pended in the bardo of dying. The word *bardo* names "a group of states"—

dying, sleeping, dreaming, and meditating—"gaps or periods in which the possibility of realization is particularly available."[4] Realization, in this sense, is different from knowledge. It is a shadow that lags behind knowing and is harder to grab onto: we know we will die, for example, but the realization of that fact is another order of achievement. Stalking victims experience a mutated, debilitating form of the awareness particular to being thrown into a state of suspense. A threat of violence seems to emanate from the fact of your being. You want to stay very still, and you also want to move. You have a heightened awareness of the fact that you do not know what is going to happen. A hypervigilance descends on you, loading you with the sense that you can never know enough, which is true. You start to feel unreal, frozen, locked into a strange and debilitating relationship with knowledge and time. This, I think, can be called a form of derealization. I think now that I have been slow to realize, in the sense Eve describes. I have felt absented from myself and have drifted out of my work.

In her archive, the most luscious writing on the subject of work and working appears in letters Eve sent to her brother David. In 1983, near his thirtieth birthday, he asked his older sister for advice about developing good "work habits." She opens a seven-page reply by declaring, "I never had any work habits at all and don't intend to."[5] From that shameless deflection, she describes a relationship to work that is scandalous for its sense of leisure. The letter is worth citing at length:

> I can't work at all unless it's <u>absolutely clear</u> (to me, to whoever's around) that if at any given moment I don't want to be working, then I will not work. It is at the level of principle, for me, to break absolutely when I wish to, for whatever—food, walk, bath, talk to self, daydream. . . . The most typical scene of me writing is the moment when I sit up straight, furrow my brow, and say to myself (<u>out loud</u>)—"Now, what do I WANT?" With the assumption that what I want, I can have. To me, this is the meaning of being grown up. ON the other hand, the framework of this, as you know, is probably a really unusually circumscribed and obsessionally-organized sphere of life, so that the actual choices are at any given moment very few—and what's probably more important, they never lead very far away from the basic concerns at hand. I mean, what I write in critical prose isn't <u>exactly</u> what I teach isn't <u>exactly</u> what I write in poetry isn't <u>exactly</u> what I talk with Hal about isn't <u>exactly</u> what I fantasy when I masturbate

isn't <u>exactly</u> what I read over dinner isn't <u>exactly</u> what my women's group discusses—but they aren't exactly a million miles apart either.[6]

This is an artist's sense of work—a mode of creative production staged close to habit, in which the work of writing is woven into the practice of living. She goes on to explain that her relationship to profession—she a poet, scholar, teacher—is not the theater through which she experienced success or failure. "My deepest definition of a successful year," she tells her brother, "is a year in which I am not depressed," a condition she describes as "too much time with too little desire": "As long as the ice (of time, desire) doesn't break, I'm accomplishing the main thing I want to accomplish, and I'm content with myself. . . . The bottom line—what makes it easy—is that successes there [in writing projects] are gravy—are pleasure, actively fun—because what I most importantly ask of the work is so very little (just to keep me off the ice)."[7] Keeping us "off the ice" is not so very little to ask of our work. As a teacher, Eve talked about these things with her students. Many of us in that community—Duke in the 1990s—were in therapy. Back then I had a tortured relationship to writing and a distorted sense of the quality of my work. When I tried to focus on it, my work felt like garbage—it made no sense, and nobody could tell me any different. When I was in that state, I was difficult to be around. I went through an awful stretch where I cried anytime I tried to talk about my dissertation. I seemed fine, but as soon as I tried to speak, tears "slipped over my lids" and mortified me. Nothing people said to me about the quality of my work was enough; no affirmation of its value was effective. I wanted so much from my work I scared myself.

After my trip to visit Eve's archive, I met Hal in New York. We walked around and around the edges of Washington Square Park, talking about the past. At some point, we lighted on the question of what Eve would have thought about #metoo, trigger warnings, and campus-based sexual harassment—so many people, on learning I was exploring her archive, had asked me this question.

She clearly understood her own story as shaped by institutional sexism. Her first academic jobs were at institutions that had only recently begun to admit women students. Files related to those early years include notes for groups centered in the welfare of women students and faculty, and memos tracing the attempt to establish courses and programs centered in feminist and gay and lesbian studies. These are mingled with talks like "Women and Language" (which opens with the observation, "there are two fantasies about women and language, which I'll call the Dumb Pussy fantasy and the Flow-of-Words fantasy"[8]) and a 1985 address to Amherst College's senior assembly in which she leaves graduating students with the following call to arms:

> We have to think seriously and openly and specifically, as a community, about what we mean by freedom from sexual harassment. First we need a good definition—a realistic and specific one, and one that takes into account the importance of the power of hierarchies that, realistically, structure a college community. Beyond that, though, we need a community-wide consciousness raising to make sure that these standards of behavior are genuinely known and understood, both by potential harassers and, perhaps even more importantly, by potential victims. In schools where this kind of attention has not been paid, enforcement of these standards has consistently proven to be capricious, arbitrary, very often racist, very often homophobic, and wildly ineffective.[9]

This, she situates as an important part of understanding and cultivating diversity. The first iteration of "The Privilege of Unknowing" was published in *Genders* in 1988. There, she describes "the epistemological asymmetry of the laws that govern rape" as a "rape machinery" that "keeps disproportionately under discipline . . . women's larger ambitions to take more control over the terms of our own circulation."[10] It took her a decade to land something we'd call security of employment in the form of a full-time, tenured position in a welcoming department. She writes about that hire in a letter to her brother. She applied to work at Amherst College three times. The first time she interviewed there, she met Liz Bruss. Bruss had been hired by Amherst College's English department in 1972, a few years before the college began admitting women students. The first woman hired into a tenure-track position in that department, she was what Amherst calls a "pioneering woman"—a member of the generation that desegregated Amherst's all-male faculty. Eve didn't see Bruss at the final round of on-campus interviews. "I heard later," she tells her brother, that "she had just had a miscarriage, her second, and was sick and depressed."[11] Eve applied a second time, for a one-year visiting position as a poet. She wasn't hired, but she was a finalist for that search and visited the campus for the last round of interviews. In conversation with faculty there, she learned that Bruss was pregnant again, thanks to a hormone treatment which might allow her to carry that baby to term. When she saw Bruss, "Liz was looking extremely lovely and happy."[12]

Bruss died very suddenly that year; she had been eight months into her pregnancy when, "in the space of a couple of hours—some tumor, or something, in her endocrine system, whose existence nobody had ever suspected, which *may* or may not have been aggravated by the hormones, or the pregnancy, but who knows, just suddenly killed her."[13] The department appealed to their dean to run a search to replace Bruss. They advertised for a position in critical theory (Bruss's field) and hired a man. *Then*, Eve wrote to her brother, they slowly realized that they hadn't replaced her at all: "Fond as they are of Andy Parker [the man they hired], they still haven't *quite* succeeded in replacing Liz—and that Liz's having been a woman, and a feminist, and over 30, may have had as much to do with her importance to them as her being a critical theorist."[14] So, they wrote a new advertisement that called for expertise in English literature and women's studies. Nearly every woman Eve knew applied for it. Word got around that the department was looking for someone not like Bruss, but "like Eve." Candidates were asked what they thought about her work. For Eve, this was distressing: "Everybody was going to be angry at me whether or not I got the job—and meanwhile," given the sexual politics of her work, she explains, "much as Amherst might say that they wanted someone like ES, obviously the chances of their wanting anyone quite as much like ES as yours truly seemed fairly slim—or, perhaps, they might want someone even *more* like ES."[15] She did manage to be just enough but not too much "Eve" for them: they hired her.

Reproductive problems abound in this account: Eve is a substitution for Liz Bruss, a replacement sought after the department (in Eve's narrative) had gotten its first attempt at that substitution wrong by not appreciating the importance of the fact that Bruss was "a woman and a feminist." But she is also filling a space carved out by an idea of "ES," which is not quite the same thing as her actual self. This chain of substitution is anchored in the grave of a woman who died in a pregnancy: Bruss's death was "a sickening shock for everybody at Amherst, since Liz was first of all a wonderful and smart person, and secondly very important to the dept.—even though, as a pioneering woman, she'd also had incredible amounts of shit from them, and there are credible older women in other departments who are willing to say that that's what really killed her."[16] In accepting this job, she stepped into the institution's ecology of grief and grievance.

When I was hired at the University of California, Riverside, the senior Americanist in my department was Emory Elliott. Emory moved to my campus from Princeton. That campus's English department had been torn apart by the university's response to a sexual assault case: a graduate student accused a faculty member of rape. The fact that the student and the faculty member were both men, combined with the department's prestige, made this into the academic scandal of the moment. The case was handled so badly that numbers of faculty, like Emory, left the campus in protest. This made national news.[17] When I started at Riverside in 1999, the dust had barely settled on terrible sexual harassment cases in our history department. In May that year, the *Chronicle of Higher Education* published an exposé titled "A History Department Implodes over Sex-Bias and a Suicide."[18] The subheading frames the crisis as one about "academic culture, gender, and measuring productivity." A group of men in the department had attempted to fire an assistant professor because she had become pregnant; a handful of graduate students had accused men in the department of propositioning them, and far worse.

We work inside wounds. At big, public, underresourced institutions like mine, we experience our workplace crises on a continuum: ridiculous teaching loads, a lack of instructional support, depressing and run-down classrooms, and gross understaffing yield a near daily sense of crisis that makes it really hard to do the imaginative, vulnerable-making work of confronting, for example, intractable bullies on your faculty. We forced N out of our graduate program, but the man who expressed openly sexist views in her hearing still works on my campus. In my view, he is a far bigger problem for our campus than N ever was.

Academic work is like this. We are compelled to find a wrong to right in our work. Many of us work on subjects that have a direct relationship to who we are and what we've been through. That's the case here: For nearly fifteen years I have been thinking about what happened, about the action of casting N out. We certainly needed a break from her crisis, which engulfed not just me but my colleagues. But her crisis resonated with deeper problems in our workplace: if I have a desire for justice around my case, it is about those cracks in the foundation.

As I write this, I move from the memory of standing in the back of the lecture hall seeing N announce Eve's death to my students, to the memory of sitting at my desk a few months later trying to talk with N about her behavior toward me. In advance of our meeting I crafted sentences that I hoped would make clear that she was important to me, that her writing and her well-being mattered to me. I tried to find a way to say *stop* without embarrassing either one of us. I invoked Eve in that conversation: I offered to be something like

Eve for her. N could only hear what I said as a disavowal imposed on me by institutional prohibition. And she wasn't wrong.

Looking back, much of what I imagined as unsayable was, actually, perfectly sayable. It should be OK to tell a student that you do not love them! What if I'd laughed, and said, *Honestly, you really aren't my type!*? And then I remember that N knew nearly all of this. She read every bit of my work. No amount of frankness was likely to help if it challenged her experience. I didn't know enough then about what she was going through. Things went so wrong not because N had an attachment to me that I could not return but because, within the institution holding us in relation to each other, we could neither recognize nor address the crisis in the relationship between her life and her work, and the way that crisis ricocheted through my own navigation of life, work, and love.[19]

Many who work in gender and sexuality studies are seeking the integration of life, work, and love that Eve described in that conversation with her therapist. "The work is *about* sex and love and desire," she explained, projecting onto Shannon, "like your work I suppose — so it's almost bound to be involving at that intimate level."[20] For some of us, for me, this way of working addresses the ongoing violence of a world that tears work and love apart. "As soon as the distribution of labor comes into being," Marx writes, "each man has a particular, exclusive sphere of activity, which is forced upon him and from which he cannot escape. He is a hunter, a fisherman, a herdsman, or a critical critic, and must remain so if he does not want to lose his means of livelihood."[21] As work is rationalized, carved up, as the value of our labor is rendered into a form that allows its extraction, "not only is the specialized work distributed among the different individuals, but the individual is himself divided up, and transformed into the automatic motor of a detail operation, thus realizing the absurd fable of Menenius Agrippa, which presents man as a mere fragment of his own body."[22] This alienation of people from their labor, this particularization of the self, "attacks the individual at the very roots of his life."[23] The dream of communism is the dream of a world in which "nobody has one exclusive sphere of activity but each can become accomplished in any branch he wishes, society regulates the general production and thus makes it possible for me to do one thing today and another tomorrow, to hunt in the morning, fish in the afternoon, rear cattle in the evening, criticize after dinner, just as I have a mind, without ever becoming hunter, fisherman, herdsman or critic."[24] Marx is fuzzy on details when it comes to articulating just how a society might regulate us all so perfectly that our labor might be liberated from the grind of the job and work dissolved into the practice of living.

That is the pleasure of the idea of Eve at her desk, leaning back from the text she is working on to ask herself, *Now, what do I want?* It's a very queer take on work, one that barely looks like work at all. The word she uses in her 1983 letter to her brother is not *queer*, however, but *sick*:

> There's <u>no</u> relation to work that is not pretty sick—whether you do it, don't do it, have insights into it, whatever. I mean, you're brought up into a gendered nuclear family under late capitalism, you're going to have a sick relation to work. I think it's important (for folks like us) to feel our way into lots of different (successful and unsuccessful, productive and unproductive) people's relations to work, and see the various sicknesses—NOT to feel disgust at them, but just to stop comparing one's own relation to work with some imagined standard of ok-ness. The point is to figure out some ways of having fun in your relation to whatever you do, figure out some (even incidental) rewards that will actually feel to you like rewards, and maybe even at best get something interesting done.[25]

Harassment makes this kind of reflection and generosity impossible. It roots itself in the pockets of alienation that capitalism requires. Sexual harassment exploits the spaces of incoherence and contradictions produced by the way our lifework is organized. Sexual harassment cases trigger the reactions they do because they force us to confront and work through those contradictions— most people can't or won't do the latter. Our workplaces handle harassment so poorly because in very real ways our labor is organized by harassment. Our instincts tell us that confronting the use of sex to separate us from our work brings us very close to the destruction of the institutions that hold our labor and give us our shape, whether that be the school, the workplace, or the family. That ideology slips into our thoughts and tells us what we can afford to do, and what we can't. It is where the word *afford* describes not only a sense of wealth and privilege but the environment that holds us along with our sense of the possibilities for our labor. It makes the idea of loving your job, loving your students, and loving, even, the school at which you work into a foolishness or, worse, an obscenity. Within that frame of mind, the violations of our love, of our trust, express not the brutality of sexed and raced forms of extraction but our stupidity.

If we cannot find happiness at work, we are expected find it at home—and the happiness of that home, for women especially, is supposed to anchor your being. Anyone who has been through it at work knows that this is a ruse: when you get home, you keep working; you can't talk about anything but work; you can't sleep. Or you shut down, you defer your whole self, waiting for a time and place when you can be who you are and do what you really want. Which is a way of saying that you stop living.

People often say, of the emotional pain of investing in one's workplace, "the institution won't love you back." This bit of common sense expresses a limited truth. An institution is a network of attachments sustained by the people who live their work through that organization. It is a thing and doesn't love or hate in and of itself. A community may lean into its sense of the institution, however, in order to deflect and channel that community's capacity for violence. Left untended, the institution will nurture the worst in people. One avoids, disavows, conducts, and amplifies abuse dynamics through a collective paralysis. The stories of cases that draw my interest as a critic get at the everyday fascism of this form of institutional life, in which a group of people reinforce their sense of workplace hierarchy and collaborate in gaslighting and abuse—and may even do so in the name of the victim's interests. In Nassar's workplace (a college campus) that collaboration was made possible by the devaluation of not just victim discourse but sexual knowledge itself. The girls and women he abused were not just silenced: they were made to apologize to him, coerced into more treatments, and shamed so that his colleagues could enjoy the libidinal payoff of social cohesion.

Earlier, in my writing about Nassar, I cited Sedgwick's interest in "the operations necessary to deploy male-male desire as the glue rather than as the solvent of a hierarchical male disciplinary order," revising the question to ask, "What are the operations necessary to deploy sex as the glue rather than as the solvent of a hierarchical disciplinary order?"[26] What happens when we slow that question down, flatten it out: When is sex the site of the consolidation and the unraveling of disciplinary order? When does that unraveling institute a simple reordering of power, and when does it open up our sense of what power is? Within our social structures, questions about sex are loaded with potential to do the latter. Within an abusive advising dynamic, sex might be the thing that shames a student into compliance with whatever the professor demands of them not only sexually, but in their work. This cements the professor's authority over, at minimum, that student—a student who is likely to be isolated, furthermore, from their cohort as that student's sexualization binds the cohort in opposition to them. The open secret of that teacher-student relationship reinforces the professor's hold on their community—the whole group is complicit in such things. Sex is also a solvent—it breaks relationships, breaks departments open—it can be the vector through which hierarchical academic communities are rearranged, not because students and teachers are fucking each other, but because that possibility is held within the group as a shame-ridden possibility. What does it mean to be present to that? To take responsibility for that possibility and for its shame? To hold that possibility with love for each other and with respect for each other? To be frank about what it means to seduce a student out of their career—a career about which so many of us are so deeply ambivalent?

People need different things from their work at different times: some of us sometimes define ourselves through our labor, feel quite unified with the work of the job, and some of us sometimes anchor that sense of self elsewhere. Some jobs are great for people who want to be at home at work, and some are great for people who need heavy boundaries between what they experience as their personal lives and their working lives. The laws that govern our workplaces address only what the state requires of us and do so through the language of prohibition and regulation. The fostering of a workplace in which harassment does not thrive requires far more than mere compliance. Antiharassment work requires that we explore how our relationships to our jobs might actually fortify our sense of pleasure, as well as our capacities for intimacy and even love. Antiharassment work requires an active and ongoing commitment to enhancing people's ability to enjoy their lives—to not only do their job, but to pleasure in it. These are a few of the things that I am still learning from Eve, and from my students.

NOTES

INTRODUCTION

1. Baum, Catalano, Rand, and Rose, "National Crime Victimization Survey," 7.

2. Spitzberg, Nicastro, and Cousins, "Exploring the Interactional Phenomenon of Stalking."

3. I take up the broad sense that sexual harassment and assault cases cannot be reported (because they can't be researched) in *Campus Sex, Campus Security*, in a brief discussion of the infamous 2014 *Rolling Stone* article, "A Rape on Campus." Jia Tolentino discusses that case in thoughtful detail in *Trick Mirror*. For a case-based analysis of the difficulty of administering sexual harassment complaints on campus, see Brodsky, *Sexual Justice*. Laura Kipnis's *Unwanted Advances* is one of the worst examples of the kind of irresponsible, harmful writing about harassment cases I am describing here. There, she briefly discusses a case in my department. Her discussion of that case is harmful.

4. Foucault, *The History of Sexuality*, 103.

5. For excellent reporting on campus-based harassment cases, see Jessica Luther and Dan Solomon's reporting of sexual harassment at Baylor University for *Texas Monthly* (e.g., Luther and Solomon, "Silence at Baylor") and Nidhi Subbaraman's reporting of an investigation at UC Santa Cruz for *BuzzFeed* (e.g., Subbaraman, "Some Called It 'Vigilante Justice'").

6. A slightly different version of this paragraph opens my foreword to Friedrich Engels's *The Origin of the Family, Private Property, and the State*, ix.

7. The difficult experiences of many women of color in the academy grow in part from being placed at great remove from these hollow forms of promise. Important publications addressing this fact include Niemann et al., *Presumed Incompetent*; and Ahmed, *On Being Included*.

8. See, for example, Smith and Freyd, "Dangerous Safe Havens."

CHAPTER ONE. ON THE DISTANCES BETWEEN US

1. The event was *Trashing Performance*, part of a three-year research program *Performance Matters*, convened by Gavin Butt, Adrian Heathfield, and the Live Art Development Agency, 2010–13. The specific event in question was a series of conversations titled *Under and Overwhelmed: Emotion and Performance*, Toynbee Theatre, London, October 26, 2011.

2. See Doyle, "Distance Relation."

3. Nancy, *Being Singular Plural*, xvi.

4. Rankine, *Citizen*, 49.

5. Nancy, *Being Singular Plural*, xvi.

6. Nancy, *Being Singular Plural*, xvi.

7. Nancy, *Being Singular Plural*, xv.

8. Unless otherwise indicated, all direct quotations from Adrian Howells are taken from a transcription of our conversation at the conference *Trashing Performance*. I have edited these passages, but only to remove small words (e.g., superfluous uses of *and*) and to better translate to the page some of the conversation's cadences. Thank you to Harriet Curtis for preparing the transcription.

9. See, for example, Hall, "Selfies and Self-Writing."

10. Heddon and Howells, "From Talking to Silence."

11. I wrote a few sentences like this in a memorial essay, "Untitled."

12. Barthes, "The Death of the Author," 142.

13. Whitman, *The Portable Walt Whitman*, 213–15.

14. Kristeva, "On the Melancholic Imaginary," 6.

15. See Kristeva, *Black Sun*.

16. Kristeva, "On the Melancholic Imaginary," 5.

17. Kristeva, "On the Melancholic Imaginary," 7.

18. Kristeva, "On the Melancholic Imaginary," 5.

19. Kristeva, "On the Melancholic Imaginary," 17.

20. Muñoz, *Cruising Utopia*, 167.

21. Thomas, "Graduate Student Discovered Dead in Durham Apartment."

22. Doyle, letter to the editor.

23. Crimp, "Mourning and Militancy," 136.

24. Crimp, "Mourning and Militancy," 140.

25. Nancy, *Being Singular Plural*, 2.

26. Nancy, *Being Singular Plural*, 42.

CHAPTER TWO. A PAIN IN THE NECK

1. It took me a while to settle on a letter to stand in for this person's name. I chose N as an abbreviation for *name*. I want to make clear: as much as N's crisis impacted me, the lasting difficulties that continue to shape my relationship with my work are the effect of the institutional setting of my case. If I were to blame

anyone or anything, it would be the combination of abusive and enabling faculty who made this difficult situation worse and an institutional culture that encourages us to imagine that policies somehow transcend the limits of the people charged with the responsibility of executing them. I am hoping that this story helps readers understand what I mean by this.

2. Legal definitions of harassment pivot on terms like *unwelcomed* and *unwanted*. In student or faculty conduct policy, for example, harassment may be defined as repeated unwanted behavior that causes a person distress. Stalking is an intensification of harassment that often leaves a victim feeling watched, surveilled, and fearful. Consensual personal or sexual relationships between a supervisor and employee or between a teacher and student present different but related problems. These relationships, at minimum, represent conflicts of interest and furthermore expose the subordinate participant to potential harassment and retaliation or accusations of having benefited unfairly from that relationship. They can birth ecologies of distrust. Universities generally either prohibit such relationships or require that they be identified, and the supervisor/teacher be recused from any evaluation of that person's work.

3. Park Dietz, cited by Rose Minutaglio in "Murdered Actress Rebecca Schaeffer's Father Speaks Out in New ABC Special."

4. When someone files a complaint against you at school, the school has to let you know. However, they may not share the specifics of the charges until you are interviewed by staff or by an investigator. This can be weeks or even months later.

5. I was told that one aim of this hearing was to establish a disciplinary record that would prevent her from enrolling in any program at my campus. I do not think such a thing is fair—if she took responsibility for and managed her stalking impulses, why shouldn't she be allowed to pursue her education? It is also ineffective: there is no sex offender registry for schools nor should there be. Furthermore, that outcome has nothing to do with my own safety (guaranteeing that she not be able to enroll at our university is not the same as guaranteeing that she would leave me alone).

6. Gideonse, "Framing Sam See."

7. At the time, people handling my case were confused about privacy regulations. It was a student disciplinary hearing, and even though it was about the fact she was stalking me (and had her behavior been less threatening, I'd have been there in person), it was not clear to staff if I had a right to know the details of what was said, given that the Federal Education Right to Privacy Act protects student disciplinary records. Even if that information had been protected by FERPA (which is debatable), once it was shared with me, I was within my rights to speak of it.

8. When faculty groom students, they sexualize their relationship to them, edging the advising relationship until it becomes something else: many sexual harassment complaints of this sort have an archive documenting this.

CHAPTER THREE. A CASE OF PARANOIA

1. "[Paranoia] has been at the center of considerable classificatory turbu-
lence, especially," writes Leo Bersani, "with respect to the question of whether
or not it should count as one of the schizophrenic psychoses. More than any
other psychoanalytic term," he continues, "*paranoia* has been the focus of a no-
sological disarray not unlike the symptomatic panic of paranoia itself. There is,
at both cases, interpretive distress." Bersani, "Pynchon, Paranoia, and Literature," 99.

2. Here, in referring to groups, I am using the language of C. Fred Alford,
who draws from Kleinian models in his writing about affect, social movements,
and political culture. Understandings of paranoia modeled after the work of
Melanie Klein use the term *paranoia* to describe the shape of a child's frustration, fear, and anxiety. Frustrated by the parent who cannot fulfill the child's
needs as those needs arise, a child will "split" parental figures into the bad parent and a good parent, or the "bad breast" and the "good breast." The steady
presence of "decent, caring, loving parents" mitigates the child's "paranoid-
schizoid fears," allowing the child to recognize that the parent is both "good"
and "bad." Alford, *Melanie Klein and Critical Social Theory*, 57. This, in
Kleinian narratives of child development, is crucial. Empathy and compassion
grow from this integrative understanding of the good and the bad in people
around us. Groups, Alford writes, "also deal with ideas of people: the idea of the
good group member or citizen, the bad Communist, the trade unionist, or the
capitalist exploiter, to name just a few" (57). Groups are, in fact, quite strongly
shaped by ideas of other people—who is in the group, and who is not; whether or
not one is recognized as a member of a group; whether members of a group understand or like you. Alford observes that groups tend to have a strong paranoid-
schizoid character and suggests that it is much more difficult for groups to work
through, integrate, and reckon with the splitting and projections generated by
the group. Such a thing can challenge a group's sense of its own identity and
well-being. This is particularly true of large groups—for example, the members
of a large university community, people belonging to a political party, and so
on. See especially the third chapter of Alford's *Melanie Klein and Critical Social
Theory*.

3. Tomkins, *Affect, Imagery, Consciousness*, 459.

4. The term *schizoid* is used to name thought/emotion systems defined by
splitting and differentiation. These processes are essential aspects of human
experience (e.g., the discovery of self/other, but also safe/dangerous, edible/
inedible). They are necessary to the formation of the self and the navigation of
basic experiences of need and frustration. They are, however, loaded with corro-
sive potential. Value systems organized around ideal and abject subjects (white/
Black; male/female; straight/gay; citizen/alien) are schizoid. An investment in
the security of these binaries yields a violent defense against any challenge to the

boundaries dividing one side from the other. Scholars who research subjects like institutional racism and misogyny work with structures that exploit and capitalize on these forms of differentiation. This is different from the set of disorders gathered under the diagnostic language of schizophrenia. For patient-centered writing about schizophrenia, see Bollas, *When the Sun Bursts*; and Weijun Wang's memoir, *The Collected Schizophrenias*.

5. Klein, "Notes on Some Schizoid Mechanisms," 2.

6. Freud, "On the Mechanism of Paranoia," 30.

7. Freud, "On the Mechanism of Paranoia," 33.

8. Freud, "A Case of Paranoia," 97. All subsequent references to this article are followed by page numbers from this edition.

9. Schor, "Female Paranoia," 150.

10. Halberstam, *Skin Shows*, 125.

11. Schor, "Female Paranoia," 154.

12. When Sedgwick asserts "queer studies has had a distinctive history of intimacy with the paranoid imperative" (*Touching Feeling*, 126) it is with the authority of a scholar who wrestled with paranoia across three book projects. Paranoia, as a mode of relation and a problem, shapes *The Coherence of Gothic Conventions* and activates the homosocial vectors of the Girardian triangles of *Between Men*. *Epistemology of the Closet* signals a major shift as, in that work, Sedgwick approaches theories of sexuality as not only knowledge systems but as theories regarding what can be known and what knowledge is. Her last sustained reflection on paranoia is a much-debated essay, "Paranoid Reading and Reparative Reading; or, You're So Paranoid You Probably Think This Introduction Is about You," published in *Touching Feeling*. See also Hocquenghem, *Homosexual Desire*, esp. 55–72; Bersani, "Pynchon, Paranoia, and Literature"; and Kurnik, "A Few Lies." The concluding third of Kurnik's essay dives into Sedgwick's and Bersani's writing on paranoia and critical practice.

13. Sedgwick, "Paranoid Reading and Reparative Reading," 126.

14. Sedgwick, *Between Men*, 16.

15. Hocquenghem, *Homosexual Desire*, 61.

16. *Revenge porn* is a problematic term: it suggests that the distribution of sexual images is an act of retribution, done to avenge a wrong.

17. See McGlynn, Rackley, and Houghton, "Beyond 'Revenge Porn'"; McGlynn et al., "'It's Torture for the Soul'"; Hearn and Hall, "This Is My Cheating Ex."

18. See Poole, "Fighting Back against Non-consensual Pornography"; Thompson and Wood, "A Media Archeology of the Creepshot"; Lake, "Watching Women."

19. Lauer, "Surveillance History and the History of New Media," 567.

20. "The Camera Epidemic," *New York Times*, August 20, 1884, 4, cited by Berger, "Photography Distinguishes Itself," 224.

21. Brandeis and Warren, "The Right to Privacy."

22. For more on this, see, for example, Siepp, "The Right to Privacy in Nineteenth-Century America."

23. Brandeis and Warren, "The Right to Privacy," 196.

24. Brandeis and Warren, "The Right to Privacy," 196.

25. "The Photographic Nuisance," 153–54.

26. See White, "Rebecca Latimore Felton and the Wife's Farm."

27. Nash, "From Lavender to Purple," 306.

28. Glissant, *Poetics of Relation*, 189–94.

29. Lauer, "Surveillance History and the History of New Media," 571.

30. Anzieu, *The Skin Ego*.

31. See Lafrance, "From the Skin Ego to the Psychic Envelope."

32. Anzieu, "Formal Signifiers and the Ego-Skin," 1.

33. Anzieu, "Formal Signifiers and the Ego-Skin," 2.

34. Anzieu, "Formal Signifiers and the Ego-Skin," 3.

35. Laing, *The Divided Self*, 37.

36. Memo written by the Student Conduct Committee summarizing the Student Conduct and Academic Integrity Program hearing, addressed to N and copied to my chair.

37. Doyle, "Blind Spots."

38. Mullen et al., "Assessing and Managing the Risks," 439.

39. Mullen et al., "Assessing and Managing the Risks," 440.

40. Ahmed, *Complaint*, 19.

41. Schor, "Female Paranoia," 152.

42. Casper, *A Handbook of the Practice of Forensic Medicine*, 253.

43. Von Krafft-Ebing, *Textbook of Insanity*, 395.

44. In the nineteenth century, this set of behaviors, taken to an extreme, was marked as a socially deviant behavior ("querulousness") and could be prosecuted in court. In the twentieth, this category of pathology faded as complaints and grievances became administrative processes within the workplace: engagement with those processes was presented as a form of corporate citizenship. Grant Lester and Patrick Mullen hypothesize that "the virtual disappearance of the querulous from the professional landscape corresponded to a period when complaints and grievance procedures were emerging as a central mechanism for resolving conflict in social systems which increasingly based their legitimacy on an ideology of individual rights. . . . A privileged few can afford to go directly to the courts, but for most complaint resolution procedures are their bulwark against the power of private and public agencies." Mullen and Lester, "Vexatious Litigants," 335. See also Benjamin Lévy's history of the concept of the querulant, "From Paranoia Querulants to Vexatious Litigants." The recognition of the litigious paranoid has been mediated by shifts in workplace practice as employees have been increasingly obliged to file complaints in order to regulate the abuse of

power in the workplace. Mullen and Lester, "Vexatious Litigants"; Freckelton, "Querulent Paranoia."

45. See Mullen and Lester, "Vexatious Litigants." I am also drawing from Lester's slide presentations (e.g., "The Unreasonable, Vexatious and Querulant").

46. Mullen and Lester, "Vexatious Litigants," 340–41.

47. Mullen and Lester, "Vexatious Litigants," 341.

48. Speaking here as a complainant: from inside the grievance process, one does not necessarily recognize one's own positionality as that of the whistleblower. If you aren't prone to (or actively resist) paranoid thinking, for example, you might minimize the importance of things like an administrator "losing" your complaint. Instead of understanding this as the suppression of a complaint that might trigger a serious unraveling of some aspect of systemic abuse, you might chalk it up to, say, understaffing or individual incompetence.

49. Mullen and Lester, "Vexatious Litigants," 341.

50. Mullen and Lester, "Vexatious Litigants," 342.

51. For more on how survivors understand justice, see Herman, *Truth and Repair*.

52. Freud, *The Schreber Case*.

53. Marx and Engels, *The Economic and Philosophical Manuscripts of 1844*, 74.

54. Marx and Engels, *The Economic and Philosophical Manuscripts of 1844*, 74.

55. Federici, "Why Sexuality Is Work," 24.

56. Federici, "Counterplanning from the Kitchen," 35.

57. Marxist feminists treat gendered divisions of labor as structures that produce contradictions which can be exploited. Unpaid and underpaid reproductive work is the site of an ongoing primitive accumulation in which, as Leopoldina Fortunati writes, "reproduction [is] posited as 'natural production,' which [enables] two workers [e.g., husband and wife] to be exploited with one wage, and the entire cost of reproduction to be unloaded onto the labor force." *The Arcane of Reproduction*, 9. The scenario that Fortunati describes is not merely that of the woman confined to wageless housework; it is that of the gendered subject who embodies the splitting of work and sex. Much as we are encouraged to imagine them in partnership, productive and reproductive labor do not form a Platonic couple; they do not add up to a whole. "This range is not a unity," Fortunati argues, "because the two segments which must add up to become . . . necessary . . . labor-power, are supplied through two valorization processes which are complete in themselves" (89). We should not think of productive and reproductive labor as two halves of a whole; one is, more nearly, a world contained in and carried by the other.

58. This is the source of much analysis and debate in feminist legal studies. See, for example, MacKinnon and Siegel, *Directions in Sexual Harassment Law*;

and Canadian legal studies scholar Faraday, "Dealing with Sexual Harassment in the Workplace."

59. Acker, "Hierarchies, Jobs, Bodies," 140.

60. Acker, "Hierarchies, Jobs, Bodies," 149.

61. Federici, "Why Sexuality Is Work," 24.

62. McGinley, *Masculinity at Work*, 6.

63. Sedgwick, *Epistemology of the Closet*, 94.

64. Freud, *Introductory Lectures on Psychoanalysis*, 330.

65. Schor, "Female Paranoia," 158.

66. Schor, "Female Paranoia," 159.

67. Schor, "Female Paranoia," 161.

68. Fortunati, *The Arcane of Reproduction*, 21.

CHAPTER FOUR. HARASSMENT AND THE PRIVILEGES OF UNKNOWING

1. A version of this essay was originally published as "Harassment and the Privilege of Unknowing: The Case of Larry Nassar" in *differences* 30, no. 1 (2019).

2. Sexual coercion is a central component to quid-pro-quo sexual harassment and has been a major aspect of employment law since the 1970s, when courts first established that employees could sue their employers for sexual harassment. The sexual harassment of students was recognized as a form of sex-based discrimination in 1980 (*Alexander v. Yale*). Ronni Alexander, one of five complainants, claimed that she had been harassed and sexually coerced by one of her teachers. Sexual harassment has fallen under the domain of Title IX governance since that case. The legal precedents for linking sexual violence to sexual harassment and discrimination within Title IX frameworks have been unfolding continuously since then, with a range of decisions expanding and limiting school liability in relation to cases of sexualized forms of harm. *Davis v. Monroe County* (1999), for example, established that student-student sexual harassment can fall under Title IX governance—this decision had major implications for schools. This is the reason so much discourse about Title IX investigation centers on accusations between students. *Gebser v. Lago Vista* (1999) and *Simpson v. the University of Colorado* (2007) helped establish "deliberate indifference" frameworks for articulating institutional liability. For informed feminist scholarship representing different political perspectives on sexual harassment, compliance, and antidiscrimination law, see MacKinnon and Siegel, *Directions in Sexual Harassment Law*. For more recent scholarship and informed commentary on Title IX, sexual violence, and harassment: Brodsky and Deutsch, "The Promise of Title IX"; Halley, "Paranoia, Feminism, Law"; Halley, "Trading the Megaphone for the Gavel"; Gerson and Suk, "The Sex Bureaucracy." Title IX is closely related

to Title VII, which amends the 1964 Civil Rights Act and bans discrimination in employment.

3. See Lewis, Schuster, and Sokolow, "Gamechangers," 5–6.

4. The bibliography of writing on discrimination, sexual misconduct, sexual violence, and higher education policy is deep and broad. There are very thoughtful critics of the administrative culture that grows up around Title IX regulation (e.g., Cantalupo and Kidder, "A Systemic Look at a Serial Problem"; Howarth, "Shame Agent"; Gerson and Suk, "The Sex Bureaucracy"); feminist scholars have long been at the leading edge of the analysis of the sexual politics of civil and criminal law (e.g., Mackinnon, *Sexual Harassment by Working Women*; Halley, *Governance Feminism*; Place, *The Guilt Project*; Shultz, "Open Statement on Sexual Harassment") as well as sexuality and pedagogy (Gallop, *Feminist Accused of Sexual Harassment*; Gilbert, *Sexuality in School*; hooks, *Teaching to Transgress*; Johnson, Pellegrini, "Pedagogy's Turn"). There is a growing body of work mapping the traumatic impact of the poor administration of sexual assault and harassment cases (Smith and Freyd, "Institutional Betrayal") and efforts to create alternatives to the criminal justice system (Chen, Dulani, and Piepzna-Samarasinha, *The Revolution Starts at Home*; Koss, Wilgus, and Williamsen, "The RESTORE Program of restorative justice for sex crimes"; Deer, *The Beginning and End of Rape*; Patterson, *Queer Sexual Violence*) and white papers issued by risk management consultants (e.g., National Council of Higher Education Risk Management). My own work on campus harassment focuses on the intersection of discourses of sexual security and campus policing (Doyle, *Campus Sex, Campus Security*).

5. Gerson and Suk, "The Sex Bureaucracy."

6. Douglas, *How Institutions Think*, 52.

7. Kozlofsky, "Nassar Accusers Wish."

8. Evans, Alesia, and Kwiatkowski, "Former USA Gymnastics Doctor Accused of Abuse."

9. I shared this work with Thomashow.

10. See, for example, the case literature for *Doe v. HarperCollins Publishers, LLC*, No. 17-CV-3688, 2018 WL 1174394, at *6 (N.D. Ill. Mar. 6, 2018). This defamation complaint was filed by the woman upon whom much of Kipnis's book is focused (Doe). Kipnis represents her as a liar, as having filed multiple complaints based on false allegations of rape, and characterizes her as hysterical. In researching her book, Kipnis never spoke with this person or, as far as I am aware, attempted to research the case upon which the book is anchored. The case was settled after the defendants failed to have the case dismissed.

11. Kang, "Ending College Sexual Assault."

12. Schuster, "MSU's Loudest Survivor Refuses to Be Silenced."

13. Mencarini, "At MSU."

14. Howarth, "Shame Agent," 718.

15. Heywood, "Battling Sexual Assault at MSU."

16. Lierman, "It's on Us."

17. Will, "Colleges Become the Victims of Progressivism."

18. Will, "Title IX"; Will, "A Train Wreck Called Title IX."

19. Mack, "ASMU Becomes Latest Group to Condemn."

20. Ahern, "Hundreds to Protest"; Grasha, "MSU Students Turn Backs."

21. Coronel, Coll, and Kravitz, "Rolling Stone and UVA."

22. Hess, "How 'Snowflake' Became America's Inescapable Tough-Guy Taunt."

23. MacDonald, "Neo-Victorianism on Campus."

24. In "Who's Afraid of Title IX?," a 2017 article addressing the distortions of law and policy circulating through public discourse on rape and Title IX, Anne McClintock presents a convincing argument that the widespread characterization of the application of Title IX to sexual assault cases as a form of government overreach "is part of a [right-wing] strategy to infiltrate academia, push back Obama-era policies, undermine collective civil rights and impose large-scale deregulation." She maps a frightening collaboration between Koch-funded groups: the far-right political group ALEC, FIRE (a right-wing free speech organization), and the antifeminist Independent Women's Forum. This campaign exploits meaningful debates about the administration of sexual life to launch a broad attack on support for public education as a whole. Misogyny and the discourse of rape are instrumentalized in the service of a decredentialization of the idea of public education itself.

25. Yoffe, "The College Rape Overcorrection."

26. Douthat, "Liberalism and the Campus Rape Tribunals."

27. Douthat, "Liberalism and the Campus Rape Tribunals."

28. Kipnis, *Unwanted Advances*, 14. Nancy Chi Cantalupo and Bill Kidder describe the rhetorical movement from the subject of sexual assault to academic freedom as a stereotype about harassment which, in discourse about Title IX, "turn[s] attention to physical conduct into discussions about speech." Cantalupo and Kidder, "A Systemic Look at a Serial Problem," 676.

29. Moore, "Report on Investigation," 3. All subsequent references to this report are followed by the page number in parentheses.

30. Mencarini, "Amanda Thomashow Who Reported Nassar."

31. Mencarini, "Attorney."

32. Smith and Wells, "Gaslighting."

33. Maine, "Hear Larry Nassar's Victims."

34. Thomashow is not the first person to file a complaint against Nassar. The earliest complaints at MSU about his behavior were made in 1997 and were expressed in disclosures to coaching staff. In 2004, Brianne Randall-Gay, then fifteen, filed a complaint with Meridian Township Police (Rambo, "Meridian Township Police Department Narrative Report"); the police did not forward her complaint to prosecutors.

35. There is more to the story of the Nassar case than I can engage in this context. For example, not long after Nassar was sentenced, William Strample, the dean under whom Nassar worked, was arrested and accused of "using his position to 'harass, discriminate, demean, sexually proposition, and sexually assault female students.'" Jesse, "MSU Knew about Ex-dean's Sex Comments." In three performance reviews (staged at five-year intervals) employees complained that he sexualized his interactions with them and with students. Each review yielded a caution and a vague commitment to monitoring Strample. The question of what monitoring might have looked like went unasked.

36. Fricker, *Epistemic Injustice*, 1.

37. Fricker, *Epistemic Injustice*, 1.

38. Fricker, *Epistemic Injustice*, 150.

39. Marcus, "Fighting Bodies, Fighting Words," 387.

40. Marcus, "Fighting Bodies, Fighting Words," 387.

41. Marcus, "Fighting Bodies, Fighting Words," 382, 386.

42. Marcus, "Fighting Bodies, Fighting Words," 387.

43. See Jordan, *The Word of a Woman*.

44. Crewe and Ichikawa, "Rape Culture and Epistemology," 259.

45. Cited by Mencarini, "MSU Hid Full Conclusions."

46. An ugly and important part of this story is the fact that as individual victims have been reconciling themselves with their experiences, they have sought out new doctors to address the injuries that brought them to Nassar's office. Victim narratives now include revelations that Nassar avoided diagnosing addressable issues, to keep victims coming back. Alexandria Neason ("The Woman Coming for Larry Nassar's Job"), reporting on the experiences of gymnast Selena Brennan, writes, "After Nassar was arrested, Angie started looking for a new doctor for her daughter—this time, a woman, because Selena didn't want to see male doctors anymore. For at least a year, Nassar had been unable to find the source of the pain. But the next sports physician Selena saw administered a single MRI and immediately offered a new diagnosis: a degenerative disc."

47. A number of victims experienced this and discussed this gaslighting in their testimony at Larry Nassar's sentencing hearing. See, for example, Spain, "Why We Victim Blame"; and Wells, "The Day a Young Gymnast Tried."

48. North, "Young Women Reported Larry Nassar"; Mack, "Nassar Victim"; Wells, "The Day a Young Gymnast Tried."

49. Fitzpatrick and Conner, "McKayla Maroney Says She Tried."

50. Wang, "Final Investigative Report," 6.

51. Bissell, "Kamerin Moore Talks."

52. Rambo, "Meridian Township Police Department Narrative Report."

53. Kozlofsky and Rahal, "Victim Confronts Nassar."

54. Bissell, "Olympian Jordyn Wieber Breaks Silence."

55. Bissell, "Amanda Thomashow Speaks."

56. Mencarini, "Nassar Recommended Expert."

57. Casarez et al., "She Reported Larry Nassar."

58. Levenson, "Larry Nassar Claimed."

59. Casarez et al., "She Reported Larry Nassar."

60. Frawley and Neumann, "An Argument for Competency-Based Training."

61. American Physical Therapy Association, "In Wake of Nassar Conviction."

62. Frawley and Neumann, "An Argument for Competency-Based Training."

63. Academy of the American Physical Therapy Association, "Internal Physical Therapy Pelvic Examination and Interventions Position Statement," January 1, 2021, https://www.aptapelvichealth.org/info/-internal-physical-therapy
-pelvic-examinations-and-interventions-position-statement.

64. Frawley and Neumann, "An Argument for Competency-Based Training"; Mize, "Nassar's Atrocities."

65. Postma et al., "Pelvic Floor Muscle Problems."

66. Rabin, "Pelvic Massage Can Be Legitimate."

67. See Owens, *Medical Bondage*; Walkowitz, *Prostitution and Victorian Society*.

68. Doyle, "Dirt Off Her Shoulders."

69. Pieper, *Sex Testing*.

70. Padawar, "The Humiliating Practice."

71. Karkazis and Jordan-Young, "The Powers of Testosterone."

72. Mulla, *The Violence of Care*, 140.

73. Mulla, *The Violence of Care*, 136–37.

74. See Gilbert, *Sexuality in School*.

75. Guattari, *Psychoanalysis and Transversality*, 111.

76. Sedgwick, "The Privilege of Unknowing," 23.

CHAPTER FIVE. ALETHURGY'S SHADOWS

1. Foucault, *The Courage of Truth*, 6. Also defined in his April 22, 1981, lecture as "a ritual procedure for bringing forth aléthas: that which is true." Foucault, *Wrong-Doing, Truth-Telling*, 39. A version of this chapter was originally published in *ELH* 87, no. 2 (2020): 325–47.

2. Foucault, *The Courage of Truth*, 7.

3. Foucault, *The Courage of Truth*, 13.

4. Foucault, *The Courage of Truth*, 135.

5. Euripides, *Ion*.

6. Foucault, *Fearless Speech*, 56.

7. Foucault, *Fearless Speech*, 56.

8. Aiskhylos [Aeschylus], "Agamemnon," 48.

9. Aiskhylos [Aeschylus], "Agamemnon," 60.

10. See Benitez, "Parrhesia, Ekmarturia and the Cassandra Dialogue."

11. Aiskhylos [Aeschylus], "Agamemnon," 47.

12. Prins, "OTOTOTOI," 182.

13. Anne Carson, introduction to Aiskhylos [Aeschylus], "Agamemnon," 4.

14. Sedgwick, *Epistemology of the Closet*, 5.

15. Johnson, *The Feminist Difference*, 137.

16. Johnson, *The Feminist Difference*, 151.

17. Kipnis, *Unwanted Advances*, 149.

18. Marcus, "Fighting Bodies, Fighting Words," 338.

19. Marcus, "Fighting Bodies, Fighting Words," 387.

20. Marcus, "Fighting Bodies, Fighting Words," 387.

21. INCITE!'s work in this area is exemplary. See https://incite-national.org/ for its history and resources for organizing.

22. Marcus, "Fighting Bodies, Fighting Words," 390.

23. De Rogatis, *Elena Ferrante's Keywords*.

24. Ferrante, *The Ones Who Leave*, 68. Hereafter abbreviated as *TOWL*.

25. Ferrante, *My Brilliant Friend*, 23. Hereafter abbreviated as *MBF*.

26. Ferrante, *The Story of the Lost Child*, 167. Hereafter abbreviated as *TSLC*.

27. Ferrante, *The Story of a New Name*, 41. Hereafter abbreviated as *TSNN*.

28. Feminist analyses of Ferrante's work tend to center on gender identity, friendship, and relationships between mothers and daughters. Strong examples include Ceccoli, "On Being Bad *and* Good," and a number of essays included in Grace Bullaro's anthology, *The Works of Elena Ferrante*. Sexuality receives comparatively less attention, with the notable exceptions of Tiziana de Rogatis's *Elena Ferrante's Keywords* (cited above) and Jill Richards's contribution to *The Ferrante Letters* ("The Queer Counterfactual"), which I discuss below.

29. Kipnis, *Unwanted Advances*, 49.

30. Lupton, "Ferrante on/as Good Sex."

31. Kipnis, *Unwanted Advances*, 50.

32. Ferrante, *TOWL*, 89.

33. Morante's approach to writing this assault is an exceptionally strong example of the alignment of rape with specific forms of psychological complexity/contradiction, as described by Frances Ferguson in her essay "Rape and the Rise of the Novel": "Psychological complexity . . . pits the stipulated mental state against one's actual mental state, so that one is able to resist without resisting, can have a mental state even in unconsciousness, and is unable to consent even if one wants to" (100).

34. Oram, "Rape, Rapture and Revision," 422.

35. Butler, *Gender Trouble*, 57–65.

36. Richards, "The Queer Counterfactual," 179.

37. I discuss the relationship between writing, lesbian desire, and loss in Alcott's novel in Doyle, "Jo March's Love Poems."

38. Richards, "The Queer Counterfactual," 195.

39. Cited by Sedgwick, "The Privilege of Unknowing," 37.

40. Sedgwick, "The Privilege of Unknowing," 44.

41. Sedgwick, "The Privilege of Unknowing," 25.

42. Sedgwick, "The Privilege of Unknowing," 47.

43. Sedgwick, "The Privilege of Unknowing," 47.

44. Sedgwick, "The Privilege of Unknowing," 51.

CONCLUSION

1. Her collection is housed at the Sally Bingham Center for Women's History and Culture at the David M. Rubenstein Rare Book and Manuscript Library, Duke University, Durham, NC.

2. Sedgwick, *A Dialogue on Love*, 23.

3. Sedgwick, *A Dialogue on Love*, 23.

4. Sedgwick, "Reality and Realization," 210.

5. Eve Kosofsky Sedgwick to David Kosofsky, May 15, 1983, 2, box 30, Eve Kosofsky Sedgwick Papers.

6. Sedgwick to Kosofsky, May 15, 1983, 2.

7. Sedgwick to Kosofsky, May 15, 1983, 3, 4–5.

8. Sedgwick, "Women and Language," n.d., box 18, Eve Kosofsky Sedgwick Papers.

9. Sedgwick, "Senior Assembly Talk," May 9, 1985, box 18, Eve Kosofsky Sedgwick Papers.

10. Sedgwick, "The Privilege of Unknowing" (1993), 24.

11. Sedgwick to David Kosofsky, May 31, 1984, 8, box 30, Eve Kosofsky Sedgwick Papers.

12. Sedgwick to Kosofsky, May 31, 1984, 8.

13. Sedgwick to Kosofsky, May 31, 1984, 8.

14. Sedgwick to Kosofsky, May 31, 1984, 8.

15. Sedgwick to Kosofsky, May 31, 1984, 6.

16. Sedgwick to Kosofsky, May 31, 1984, 8.

17. See King, "4 Scholars Quit as Sex Incident Splits Princeton"; Rabinowitz, "Arms and the Man." See also Smith, *Nemesis*; this mystery novel published under Joyce Carol Oates's nom de plume is loosely inspired by the case at Princeton (where Oates worked at the time).

18. Leatherman, "A History Department Implodes."

19. Esmé Weijun Wang writes about her experiences as a student suffering from schizoaffective disorder in *The Collected Schizophrenias*: this is an important book for teachers and administrators keen to support students suffering from mental illness. It is not my place to slap a diagnosis on N, but the experience led me to learn about schizoaffective disorders and the experience of delusions. Anosognosia (the inability to know one's own disease) can be a feature of a

range of mental illnesses, as well as in dementia and as an effect of brain injury. Telling a person that they are deluded can be quite harmful. The National Alliance on Mental Illness recommends using LEAP, a supportive conversational technique that emphasizes listening, empathizing, agreeing, partnering.

20. Sedgwick, *A Dialogue on Love*, 23.

21. Marx and Engels, *The German Ideology*, 53.

22. Marx, *Capital*, 481–82.

23. Marx, *Capital*, 484.

24. Marx and Engels, *The German Ideology*, 53.

25. Sedgwick to Kosofsky, May 15, 1983, 2.

26. Sedgwick, *Epistemology of the Closet*, 94.

BIBLIOGRAPHY

Acker, Joan. "Hierarchies, Jobs, Bodies: A Theory of Gendered Organizations." *Gender and Society* 4, no. 2 (1990): 139–58.

Ahern, Louise Knott. "Hundreds to Protest Michigan State Commencement Speaker." *Lansing State Journal*, December 10, 2014.

Ahmed, Sara. *Complaint!* Durham, NC: Duke University Press, 2021.

Ahmed, Sara. *On Being Included: Racism and Diversity in Institutional Life.* Durham, NC: Duke University Press, 2012.

Ahmed, Sara. "The Problem of Perception." Feminist Killjoys, February 17, 2014. https://feministkilljoys.com/2014/02/17/the-problem-of-perception/.

Ahmed, Shireen, Amira Rose Davis, Brenda Elsey, Lindsay Gibbs, and Jessica Luther, hosts. "The Women Who Brought Down Larry Nasser (Trigger Warning)." *Burn It All Down*, episode 31, December 5, 2017.

Aiskhylos [Aeschylus]. "Agamemnon." In *An Oresteia*, edited and translated by Anne Carson, 9–74. New York: Farrar, Straus and Giroux, 2009.

Alford, C. F. *Melanie Klein and Critical Social Theory: An Account of Art, Politics, and Reason Based on Her Social Theory*. New Haven, CT: Yale University Press, 1989.

American Physical Therapy Association. "In Wake of Nassar Conviction, PT Points to Need for Education on Legitimate Pelvic Physical Therapy." American Physical Therapy Association, January 31, 2018. https://www.apta.org/news/2018/01/31/in-wake-of-nassar-conviction-pt-points-to-need-for-patient-education-on-legitimate-pelvic-physical-therapy.

Anzieu, Didier. "Formal Signifiers and the Ego-Skin." In *Psychic Envelopes*, edited by Didier Anzier, translated by Daphne Briggs, 1–26. London: Karnac, 1990.

Anzieu, Didier. *The Skin Ego: A Psychoanalytic Approach to the Self.* Translated by Naomi Segal. London: Routledge, 2018.

Barr, John, and Dan Murphy. "Nassar Surrounded by Adults Who Enabled His Predatory Behavior." *ESPN*, January 16, 2018.

Barthes, Roland. "The Death of the Author." In *Image Music Text*, edited and translated by Stephen Heath, 142–48. New York: Harper Collins, 1977.

Baum, Katrina, Shannan Catalano, Michael Rand, and Kristina Rose. "National Crime Victimization Survey: Stalking Victimization in the United States." Washington, DC: US Department of Justice, Bureau of Justice Statistics, 2009.

Benitez, Rick. "Parrhesia, Ekmarturia and the Cassandra Dialogue in Aeschuy-lus' *Agamemnon.*" *Modern Greek Studies (Australia and New Zealand): A Journal for Greek Letters* 13 (2003): 334–46.

Berger, Lynn. "Photography Distinguishes Itself: Law and the Emerging Profession of Photography in the Nineteenth-Century United States." PhD diss., Columbia University, 2016.

Bersani, Leo. "Pynchon, Paranoia, and Literature." *Critical Inquiry* 89, no. 25 (1989): 99–118.

Bissell, Joel. "Amanda Thomashow Speaks about Filing a MSU Title IX Report against Larry Nassar in 2014." *MLive*, January 17, 2018. https://youtu.b/teR7QaOrUQ8.

Bissell, Joel. "Kamerin Moore Talks about Being Larry Nassar's 'Guinea Pig' during Sentencing." *MLive*, January 22, 2018. https://youtu.be/FjB0u27J4xU.

Bissell, Joel. "Olympian Jordyn Wieber Breaks Silence as She Confronts Larry Nassar." *MLive*, January 19, 2018. https://youtu.be/Tsdz_-m9uLE.

Bollas, Christopher. *When the Sun Bursts: The Enigma of Schizophrenia*. New Haven, CT: Yale University Press, 2016.

Brandeis, Louis D., and Samuel D. Warren Jr. "The Right to Privacy." *Harvard Law Review* (1890) 4, no. 5: 193–220.

Brodsky, Alexandra. *Sexual Justice: Supporting Victims, Ensuring Due Process*. New York: Macmillan, 2021.

Brodsky, Alexandra, and Elizabeth Deutsch. "The Promise of Title IX: Sexual Violence and the Law." *Dissent* 62, no. 4 (2015): 135–44.

Bullaro, Grace, ed. *The Works of Elena Ferrante: Reconfiguring the Margins*. New York: Palgrave Macmillan, 2016.

Butler, Judith. *Gender Trouble: Feminism and the Subversion of Gender Identity*. New York: Routledge, 1990.

Cantalupo, Nancy Chi, and Bill Kidder. "A Systemic Look at a Serial Problem: Sexual Harassment of Students by University Faculty." *Utah Law Review*, no. 3 (2018): 678–786.

Casarez, Jean, Emanuella Grinberg, Sonia Moghe, and Linh Tran. "She Reported Larry Nassar in 2014. Nothing Happened." *CNN*, February 1, 2018. https://www.cnn.com/2018/02/01/us/msu-amanda-thomashow-complaint-larry-nassar/index.html.

Casper, Johann Ludwig. *A Handbook of the Practice of Forensic Medicine: Biological Division*. Translated by George William Balfour. London: New Sydenham Society, 1861.

Ceccoli, Velleda. "On Being Bad *and* Good: My Brilliant Friend Muriel Dimen." *Studies in Gender and Sexuality* 18, no. 2 (2017): 110–14.

Chen, Ching-In, Jai Dulani, and Leah Lakshmi Piepzna-Samarasinha, eds. *The Revolution Starts at Home: Confronting Intimate Violence within Activist Communities*. 2nd ed. Chico, CA: AK Press, 2016.

Coronel, Sheila, Steve Coll, and Derek Kravitz. "Rolling Stone and UVA: The Columbia University Graduate School of Journalism Report." *Rolling Stone*, April 5, 2015.

Crewe, Briana, and Jonathan Jenkins Ichikawa. "Rape Culture and Epistemology." In *Applied Epistemology*, edited by Jennifer Lackey, 253–82. Oxford: Oxford University Press, 2021.

Crimp, Douglas. "Morning and Militancy." In *Melancholia and Moralism: Essays on AIDS and Queer Politics*, 1293–49. Cambridge, MA: MIT Press, 2004.

Deer, Sarah. *The Beginning and End of Rape: Confronting Sexual Violence in America*. Minneapolis: University of Minnesota Press, 2017.

de Rogatis, Tiziana. *Elena Ferrante's Keywords*. Translated by Will Schutt. New York: Europa Editions, 2019.

Doane, Mary Ann. *The Desire to Desire: The Woman's Film of the 1940s*. Bloomington: Indiana University Press, 1987.

Douglas, Mary. *How Institutions Think*. Syracuse, NY: Syracuse University Press, 1986.

Douthat, Ross. "Liberalism and the Campus Rape Tribunals." *New York Times*, September 13, 2017.

Doyle, Jennifer. "Blind Spots." *Qui Parle* 18, no. 1 (2009): 25–52.

Doyle, Jennifer. *Campus Sex, Campus Security*. Los Angeles: Semiotext(e), 2015.

Doyle, Jennifer. "Dirt Off Her Shoulders." *GLQ: A JOURNAL OF LESBIAN AND GAY STUDIES* 19, NO. 4 (2013): 419–33.

Doyle, Jennifer. "Distance Relation: On Being with Adrian." In *It's All Allowed: The Performances of Adrian Howells*, edited by Deirdre Heddon and Dominic Johnson, 305–19. London: Intellect, 2016.

Doyle, Jennifer. Foreword to *The Origin of the Family, Private Property, and the State*, by Friedrich Engels, ix–xxvi. New York: Verso, 2021.

Doyle, Jennifer. *Hold It against Me: Difficulty and Emotion in Contemporary Art*. Durham, NC: Duke University Press, 2013.

Doyle, Jennifer. "Jo March's Love Poems." *Nineteenth-Century Literature* 60, no. 3 (2005): 375–402.

Doyle, Jennifer. Letter to the editor. *Duke Chronicle*, October 23, 1997. https://www.dukechronicle.com/article/1997/10/suicide-elicited-grossly-insensitive-coverage.

Doyle, Jennifer. "Untitled." *Social Text* 32, no. 4 (2014): 27–31.

Euripides. *Ion*. Translated by Robert Potter. Internet Classics Archive. Accessed September 12, 2023. http://classics.mit.edu/Euripides/ion.html.

Evans, Tim, Mark Alesia, and Marisa Kwiatkowski. "Former USA Gymnastics Doctor Accused of Abuse." *Indy Star*, September 12, 2016.

Faraday, Faye. "Dealing with Sexual Harassment in the Workplace: The Promise and Limitations of Human Rights Discourse." *Osgood Hall Law Journal* 32, no. 1 (1994): 33–64.

Federici, Silvia. *Caliban and the Witch: Women, the Body and Primitive Accumulation*. Rev. ed. New York: Autonomedia, 2014.

Federici, Silvia. "Counterplanning from the Kitchen." In *Revolution at Point Zero: Housework, Reproduction, and Feminist Struggle*, 28–40. Oakland, CA: PM Press, 2002.

Federici, Silvia. "Why Sexuality Is Work." In *Revolution at Point Zero: Housework, Reproduction, and Feminist Struggle*, 23–27. Oakland, CA: PM Press, 2002.

Ferguson, Frances. "Rape and the Rise of the Novel." *Representations* 152, no. 20 (1987): 88–112.

Fitzpatrick, Sarah, and Tracy Conner. "McKayla Maroney Says She Tried to Raise the Sex Abuse Alarm in 2011." *NBC News*, April 22, 2018. https://www.nbcnews.com/news/us-news/mckayla-maroney-says-she-tried-raise-sex-abuse-alarm-2011-n867911.

Fortunati, Leopoldina. *The Arcane of Reproduction: Housework, Prostitution, Labor and Capital*. Edited by Jim Fleming. Translated by Hilary Creek. New York: Autonomedia, 1995.

Foucault, Michel. *The Courage of Truth: The Government of Self and Others II: Lectures at the Collège de France, 1983–1984*. Edited by Frederic Gros. Translated by Graham Burchel. New York: Palgrave, 2011.

Foucault, Michel. *Fearless Speech*. Edited by Joseph Pearson. Los Angeles: Semiotext(e), 2001.

Foucault, Michel. *The History of Sexuality, Vol. 1: An Introduction*. Translated by Robert Hurley. New York: Vintage, 1990.

Foucault, Michel. *Wrong-Doing, Truth-Telling: The Function of Avowal in Justice*. Edited by Fabienne Brion and Bernard E. Harcourt. Translated by Stephen Sawyer. Chicago: University of Chicago Press, 2014.

Frawley, Helena C., and Patricia Neumann. "An Argument for Competency-Based Training in Pelvic Floor Physiotherapy Practice." *Physiotherapy Theory and Practice: An International Journal of Physical Therapy* 35, no. 12 (2019): 1117–30.

Freckelton, Ian. "Querulent Paranoia and the Vexatious Complainant." *International Journal of Law and Psychiatry* 11 (1988): 127–43.

Freud, Sigmund. "A Case of Paranoia Running Counter to the Theory of the

Disease." In *Sexuality and the Psychology of Love*, edited by Philip Rieff, 97–106. New York: Collier, 1963.

Freud, Sigmund. *Introductory Lectures on Psychoanalysis*. Edited and translated by James Strachey. New York: Norton, 1966.

Freud, Sigmund. "On the Mechanism of Paranoia." In *General Psychological Theory*, edited by Philip Rieff, 29–48. New York: Collier, 1961.

Freud, Sigmund. "The Sense of Symptoms." In *The Standard Edition of the Complete Psychological Works of Sigmund Freud*, edited by James Strachey, 264–69. London: Hogarth, 1966.

Freud, Sigmund. *The Schreber Case*. Translated by Andrew Webber. New York: Penguin, 2003.

Fricker, Miranda. *Epistemic Injustice*. Oxford: Oxford University Press, 2007.

Furgeson, Francis. "Rape and the Rise of the Novel." *Representations*, no. 20 (1987): 88–112.

Gallop, Jane. *Feminist Accused of Sexual Harassment*. Durham, NC: Duke University Press, 1997.

Gerson, Jacob, and Jeannie Suk. "The Sex Bureaucracy." *California Law Review* 104 (2016): 881–948.

Gideonse, Theodore K. 2016. "Framing Sam See: The Discursive Detritus of the Moral Panic over the 'Double Epidemic' of Methamphetamines and HIV among Gay Men." *International Journal of Drug Policy* 28 (2016): 98–105.

Gilbert, Jennifer. *Sexuality in School: The Limits of Education*. Minneapolis: University of Minnesota Press, 2014.

Glissant, Édouard. *Poetics of Relation*. Translated by Betsy Wing. Ann Arbor: University of Michigan Press, 1997.

Grasha, Kevin. "MSU Students Turn Backs on George Will at Commencement." *Lansing State Journal*, December 13, 2014.

Grossman, Joanna L. "Moving Forward Looking Back: A Retrospective on Sexual Harassment Law." *Boston Law Review* 95, no. 3 (2015): 1029–49.

Guattari, Félix. *Psychoanalysis and Transversality: Texts and Interviews 1955–1971*. Translated by Ames Hodges. Los Angeles: Semiotext(e), 2015.

Halberstam, J. Jack. *Skin Shows: Gothic Horror and the Technology of Monsters*. Durham, NC: Duke University Press, 1995.

Hall, Kimberly. "Selfies and Self-Writing: Cue Card Confessions as Social Media Technologies of the Self." *Television and New Media Studies* 17, no. 3 (2015): 1–15.

Halley, Janet. "Paranoia, Feminism, Law: Reflections on the Possibilities for Queer Legal Studies." In *New Directions in Law and Literature*, edited by Elizabeth S. Anker and Bernadette Meyler, 123–43. New York: Oxford University Press, 2017.

Halley, Janet. "Sexuality Harassment." In *Left Legalism, Left Critique*, edited by Janet Halley and Wendy Brown, 80–104. Durham, NC: Duke University Press, 2002.

Halley, Janet. "Trading the Megaphone for the Gavel in Title IX Enforcement." *Harvard Law Review* 128, no. 103 (2015): 103–17.

Halley, Janet, Prabha Kotiswaran, Rachel Rebouché, and Hila Shamir. *Governance Feminism: An Introduction*. Minneapolis: University of Minnesota Press, 2018.

Hearn, Jeff, and Matthew Hall. "'This Is My Cheating Ex': Gender and Sexuality in Revenge Porn." *Sexualities* 22, no. 5–6 (2019): 860–82.

Heddon, Deirdre, and Adrian Howells. "From Talking to Silence: A Confessional Journey." *PAJ: A Journal of Performance and Art* 33, no. 1 (2007): 1–12.

Heddon, Deirdre, and Dominic Johnson, eds. *It's All Allowed: The Performances of Adrian Howells*. London: Intellect, 2016.

Herman, Judith. *Truth and Repair: How Trauma Survivors Envision Justice*. New York: Basic Books, 2023.

Hess, Amanda. "How 'Snowflake' Became America's Inescapable Tough-Guy Taunt." *New York Times*, June 13, 2017.

Heywood, Todd. "Battling Sexual Assault at MSU." *Lansing State Journal*, April 2, 2014.

Hocquenghem, Guy. *Homosexual Desire*. Durham, NC: Duke University Press, 1993.

hooks, bell. *Teaching to Transgress: Education and the Practice of Freedom*. New York: Routledge, 1994.

Howarth, Joan W. "Shame Agent." *Journal of Legal Education* 66 (2017): 717–18.

Howley, Kerry. "How Did Larry Nassar Deceive So Many for So Long?" *Cut*, November 12, 2018.

Jenks, Emily. "Student Section Booing 'It's on Us' Campaign Ad Is Disrespectful." *State News*, October 7, 2014.

Jesse, David. "Michigan State Sues Insurers Seeking Payment for Nassar Settlement." *Detroit Free Press*, July 27, 2018.

Jesse, David. "MSU Knew about Ex-dean's Sex Comments in '05. It Didn't End There." *Detroit Free Press*, May 10, 2018.

Johnson, Barbara. *The Feminist Difference*. Cambridge, MA: Harvard University Press, 1998.

Johnson, Barbara. "Teaching Ignorance: *L'école des femmes*." *Yale French Studies* 63 (1982): 166–82.

Jordan, Jan. *The Word of a Woman: Police, Rape and Belief*. New York: Palgrave Macmillan, 2004.

Kang, Jay Caspian. "Ending College Sexual Assault." *Harper's*, September 9, 2014.

Karkazis, Katrina, and Rebecca M. Jordan-Young. "The Powers of Testosterone:

Obscuring Race and Regional Bias in the Regulation of Women Athletes."
Feminist Formations 30, no. 2 (2018): 1–39.

King, Wayne. "4 Scholars Quit as Sex Incident Splits Princeton." *New York Times*, May 10, 1989, Section B, 1.

Kipnis, Laura. *Unwanted Advances: Sexual Paranoia Comes to Campus*. New York: Harper and Row, 2017.

Klein, Melanie. "Notes on Some Schizoid Mechanisms." In *Envy and Gratitude and Other Works, 1946–1963*. Vol. 3 of *The Writings of Melanie Klein*, 1–24. New York: Macmillan, 1975.

Koss, Mary P., Jay Wilgus, and Kaaren M. Williamsen. "Campus Sexual Misconduct: Restorative Justice Approaches to Enhance Compliance with Title IX Guidance." *Trauma, Violence, and Abuse* 15, no. 3 (2014): 242–57.

Kozlofsky, Kim. "Nassar Accusers Wish MSU Deal Included Apology." *Detroit News*, June 4, 2018.

Kozlofsky, Kim. "What MSU Knew: 14 Were Warned of Nassar Abuse." *Detroit News*, January 18, 2018.

Kozlofsky, Kim, and Sarah Rahal. "Victim Confronts Nassar: 'Why Should We Forgive You?'" *Detroit News*, January 19, 2018.

Kristeva, Julia. *Black Sun: Depression and Melancholia*. Translated by Leon S. Roudiez. New York: Columbia University Press, 1992.

Kristeva, Julia. "On the Melancholic Imaginary." *New Formations* 3 (1987): 5–18.

Kurnik, David. "A Few Lies: Queer Theory and Our Method Melodramas." *ELH* 87, no. 2 (2020): 349–74.

Kwiatkosky, Marisa, Mark Alesia, and Tim Evans. "A Blind Eye to Sex Abuse: How USA Gymnastics Failed to Report Cases." *Indy Star*, August 4, 2016.

Lafrance, Marc. "From the Skin Ego to the Psychic Envelope: An Introduction to the Work of Didier Anzieu." In *Skin, Culture and Psychoanalysis*, edited by Sheila L. Cavanagh, Angela Failler, and Rachel Alpha Johnston Hurst, 16–44. New York: Palgrave Macmillan, 2013.

Laing, R. D. *The Divided Self: An Existential Study in Sanity and Madness*. New York: Penguin, 1990.

Lake, Jessica. "Watching Women: Past and Present Legal Responses to the Unauthorized Circulation of Personal Images." *Media and Arts Law Review* 21, no. 3 (2016).

Lauer, Josh. "Surveillance History and the History of New Media: An Evidential Paradigm." *New Media and Society* 14, no. 1 (2011): 566–82.

Lay, Sierra. "University Dedicates Thursday to Sexual Assault Education." *State News*, April 17, 2014.

Leatherman, Courtney. "A History Department Implodes over Sex-Bias and a Suicide." *Chronicle of Higher Education*, May 7, 1999.

LeBlanc, Beth. "2004 Police Report: Teen Felt 'Uncomfortable,' 'Scared,' after Nassar Appointment." *Lansing State Journal*, February 1, 2018.

Lester, Grant. "The Unreasonable, Vexatious and Querulant as Client, Employee or Spouse." Slideshow, accessed September 11, 2023. https://aicla.org/wp -content/uploads/06-DrLester_Techniques-for-Dealing-with-Difficult -Claimants.pdf.

Levenson, Eric. "Larry Nassar Claimed He Was 'the Body Whisperer' in Police Interview." *CNN*, February 2, 2018.

Lévy, Benjamin. "From Paranoia Querulants to Vexatious Litigants: A Short Study on Madness between Psychiatry and the Law, Part I." *History of Psychiatry* 25, no. 3 (2014): 299–316.

Lewis, W. Scott, Saundra K. Schuster, and Brett Sokolow. "Gamechangers: Reshaping Campus Misconduct through Litigation." National Council for Higher Education Risk Management, 2010. https://cdn.tngconsulting.com /website-media/ncherm.org/unoffloaded/2017/08/2010NCHERMWhite paper.pdf.

Lierman, Kyle. "It's on Us, a Growing Movement to End Campus Sexual Assault." *White House: President Barack Obama* (blog), September 24, 2014. https://obamawhitehouse.archives.gov/blog/2014/09/24/its-us -growing-movement-end-campus-sexual-assault.

Lukianodd, Greg, and Jonathan Heidt. "The Coddling of the American Mind." *Atlantic*, September 2015.

Lupton, Christina. "Ferrante on/as Good Sex." *ASAP Journal*, July 20, 2017. http://asapjournal.com/ferrante-onas-good-sex-christina-lupton/.

Luther, Jessica. *Unsportsmanlike Conduct: College Football and the Politics of Rape*. New York: Edge of Sports/Akashic, 2016.

Luther, Jessica, and Dan Solomon. "Silence at Baylor." *Texas Monthly*, August 20, 2015. https://www.texasmonthly.com/arts-entertainment/silence -at-baylor/.

MacDonald, Heather. "Neo-Victorianism on Campus." *Washington Examiner*, October 20, 2014.

Mack, Cameron. "ASMU Becomes Latest Group to Condemn George Will's Appearance." *State News*, December 9, 2014.

Mack, Julie. "Nassar Victim Describes Telling MSU Coach in 1997 about Abuse." *MLive*, January 20, 2018.

MacKinnon, Catherine A. *Feminism Unmodified: Discourses on Life and Law*. Cambridge, MA: Harvard University Press, 1987.

MacKinnon, Catharine A. *Sexual Harassment of Working Women: A Case of Sex Discrimination*. New Haven, CT: Yale University Press, 1979.

MacKinnon, Catharine A., and Reva B. Siegel, eds. *Directions in Sexual Harassment Law*. New Haven, CT: Yale University Press, 2014.

Maine, D'Arcy. "Hear Larry Nassar's Victims in Their Own (Brave and Powerful) Words." *espnW*, January 18, 2018. https://www.espn.com/espnw/voices

/story/_/id/22145563/hear-larry-nassar-victims-their-own-powerful
-brave-words.

Marcus, Sharon. "Fighting Bodies, Fighting Words: A Theory and Politics of
Rape Prevention." In *Feminists Theorize the Political*, edited by Judith Butler and Joan Wallach Scott, 385–403. New York: Routledge, 2002.

Marx, Karl. *Capital; Vol. 1.* Translated by Ben Fowke. New York: Knopf, 1989.

Marx, Karl, and Friedrich Engels. *The Economic and Philosophical Manuscripts
of 1844.* Edited by Dirk J. Struik. Translated by Martin Milligan. New York:
International Publishers, 1964.

Marx, Karl, and Friedrich Engels. *The German Ideology.* Edited by C. J. Arthur.
New York: International Publishers, 1970.

McClintock, Anne. "Who's Afraid of Title IX?" *Jacobin*, October 24, 2017.

McGinley, Ann. *Masculinity at Work: Employment Discrimination through a
Different Lens.* New York: New York University Press, 2016.

McGlynn, Clare, Kelly Johnson, Erika Rackley, Nicola Henry, Nicola Gavey,
Asher Flynn, and Anastasia Powell. "'It's Torture for the Soul': The Harms
of Image-Based Sexual Abuse." *Social and Legal Studies* 30, no. 4 (2021):
541–62.

McGlynn, Clare, Erika Rackley, and Ruth Houghton. "Beyond 'Revenge Porn':
The Continuum of Image-Based Sexual Abuse." *Feminist Legal Studies* 25
(2017): 25–46.

Mencarini, Matt. "Amanda Thomashow Who Reported Nassar in 2014: 'It Destroyed Me but I Lived.'" *Lansing State Journal*, January 16, 2018.

Mencarini, Matt. "Attorney: MSU Failed to 'Adequately Investigate' Nassar Complaint." *Lansing State Journal*, March 20, 2017.

Mencarini, Matt. "At MSU: Assault, Harassment, and Secrecy." *Lansing State
Journal*, December 15, 2016.

Mencarini, Matt. "MSU Hid Full Conclusions of 2014 Nassar Report from Victim." *Lansing State Journal*, January 26, 2018.

Mencarini, Matt. "Nassar Recommended Expert Who Helped Clear Him in
2014." *Lansing State Journal*, April 10, 2017.

Minutaglio, Rose. "Murdered Actress Rebecca Schaeffer's Father Speaks Out in
New ABC Special." *Elle*, April 11, 2019.

Mize, Lori. "Nassar's Atrocities Stigmatize a Legitimate Medical Treatment."
Huffington Post, January 24, 2018.

Moore, Kristine. "Report on Investigation into Allegations of Sexual Harassment: Claimant Final Report." East Lansing: Office for Inclusion and Inter-
cultural Initiatives, Michigan State University, July 18, 2014.

Morante, Elsa. *History: A Novel*, translated by William Weaver. South Royalton,
VT: Steerforth Press, 2000.

Mukomel, Lynsey. "Secret Report: Nassar's Actions Caused 'Trauma.'" *WoodTV*,

March 9, 2018. https://www.woodtv.com/news/michigan/secret-report
-nassars-actions-caused-trauma/1026866960.

Mulla, Sameena. *The Violence of Care: Rape Victims, Forensic Nurses, and Sexual Assault Intervention*. New York: New York University Press, 2014.

Mullen, Paul E., and Grant Lester. "Vexatious Litigants and Unusually Persistent Complainants and Petitioners: From Querulous Paranoia to Querulous Behavior." *Behavior Sciences and the Law* 24, no. 3 (2006): 333–49.

Mullen, Paul, Rachel Mackenzie, James Ogloff, Michele Pathé, Troy McEwan, and Rosemary Purcell. "Assessing and Managing the Risks in the Stalking Situation." *Journal of the American Academy of Psychiatry and the Law* 34, no. 4 (2006): 439–50.

Muñoz, José. *Cruising Utopia*. New York: New York University Press, 2009.

Nancy, Jean-Luc. *Being Singular Plural*. Translated by Robert D. Richardson and Anne E. O'Byrne. Stanford, CA: Stanford University Press, 2000.

Nash, Jennifer. "From Lavender to Purple: Privacy, Black Women, and Feminist Legal Theory." *Cardozo Women's Law Journal* 11, no. 2 (2005): 303–30.

Neason, Alexandria. "The Woman Coming for Larry Nassar's Job." *Bleacher Report*, July 19, 2018. https://bleacherreport.com/articles/2786857-the
-woman-coming-for-larry-nassars-job.

Niemann, Yolanda Flores, Gabriella Gutiérrez y Muhs, Carmen G. González, and Angela P. Harris, eds. *Presumed Incompetent: Race, Class, Power, and Resistance of Women in Academia*. Logan: Utah State University Press, 2020.

North, Amanda. "Young Women Reported Larry Nassar for Years. No One Took Them Seriously until Now." *Vox*, January 25, 2018.

Oram, Lydia M. "Rape, Rapture and Revision: Visionary Imagery and Historical Reconstruction in Elsa Morante's *La Storia*." *Forum Italicum: A Journal of Italian Studies* 37, no. 2 (2003): 409–35.

Owens, Deirdre Cooper. *Medical Bondage: Race, Gender, and the Origins of American Gynecology*. Atlanta: University of Georgia Press, 2017.

Padawar, Ruth. "The Humiliating Practice of Sex-Testing Female Athletes." *New York Times*, June 28, 2016.

Patterson, Jennifer, ed. *Queer Sexual Violence: Radical Voices from within the Antiviolence Movement*. New York: Riverdale Avenue, 2016.

Pellegrini, Ann. "Pedagogy's Turn: Observations on Students, Teachers, and Transference-Love." *Critical Inquiry* 25, no. 3 (1999): 617–25.

"The Photographic Nuisance." *Nation*, February 20, 1890, 153–54.

Pieper, Lindsay Parks. *Sex Testing: Gender Policing in Women's Sports*. Urbana: University of Illinois Press, 2016.

Place, Vanessa. *The Guilt Project: Rape, Morality, and the Law*. New York: Other Press, 2010.

Poole, Emily. "Fighting Back against Non-consensual Pornography." *University of San Francisco Law Review* 49, no. 1 (2015): 181–214.

Postma, Rienke, Iva Bicanic, Huub van der Vaart, and Ellen Laan. "Pelvic Floor Muscle Problems Mediate Sexual Problems in Young Adult Rape Victims." *Journal of Sexual Medicine* 10, no. 8 (2013): 1978–87.

Prins, Yopie. "OTOTOTOI: Virginia Woolf and the Naked Cry of Cassandra." In *Agamemnon in Performance: 458 BC to AD 2004*, edited by Fiona Macintosh, Pantelis Michelakis, Edith Hall, and Oliver Taplin, 163–85. New York: Oxford University Press, 2005.

Rabin, Roni Caryn. "Pelvic Massage Can Be Legitimate but Not in Larry Nassar's Hands." *New York Times*, January 31, 2018.

Rabinowitz, Dorothy. "Arms and the Man: A Sex Scandal Rocks Princeton." *New Yorker*, July 17, 1989, 30–36.

Rahal, Sarah, and Kim Kozlowski. "204 Impact Statements, 9 Days, 2 Counties, a Life Sentence for Larry Nassar." *Detroit News*, January 16, 2018.

Rambo, Paul. "Meridian Township Police Department Narrative Report: Incident 04-18086." September 17, 2004.

Randolph, Mary, and Diane M. Reddy. "Sexual Abuse and Sexual Functioning in a Chronic Pelvic Pain Sample." *Journal of Child Sexual Abuse* 15, no. 3 (2006): 61–78.

Rankine, Claudia. *Citizen: An American Lyric*. Minneapolis: Graywolf, 2014.

Richards, Jill. 2020. "The Queer Counterfactual." In *The Ferrante Letters: An Experiment in Collective Criticism*, edited by Sarah Chihaya, Merve Emre, Katherine Hill, and Jill Richards, 178–206. New York: Columbia University Press, 2020.

Schor, Naomi. "Female Paranoia." In *Breaking the Chain: Women, Theory, and French Realist Fiction*. New York: Columbia University Press, 1985.

Schultz, Vicki. "Open Statement on Sexual Harassment from Employment Discrimination Law Scholars." *Stanford Law Review* 71 (June 2018). https://www.stanfordlawreview.org/online/open-statement-on-sexual -harassment-from-employment-discrimination-law-scholars/.

Schuster, Simon. "MSU's Loudest Survivor Refuses to Be Silenced." *State News*, February 4, 2015.

Sedgwick, Eve Kosofsky. *Between Men: English Literature and Male Homosocial Desire*. New York: Columbia University Press, 1985.

Sedgwick, Eve Kosofsky. *The Coherence of Gothic Conventions*. New York: Methuen, 1986.

Sedgwick, Eve Kosofsky. *A Dialogue on Love*. Boston: Beacon, 2000.

Sedgwick, Eve Kosofsky. *Epistemology of the Closet*. Berkeley: University of California Press, 1990.

Sedgwick, Eve Kosofsky. "The Privilege of Unknowing: Diderot's *The Nun*." In *Tendencies*, 23–51. Durham, NC: Duke University Press, 1993.

Sedgwick, Eve Kosofsky. "Reality and Realization." In *The Weather in Proust*, edited by Jonathan Goldberg and Michael Moon, 206–16. Durham, NC: Duke University Press, 2011.

Sedgwick, Eve Kosofsky. *Touching Feeling: Affect, Pedagogy, Performativity.* Durham, NC: Duke University Press, 2003.

Siepp, David J. "The Right to Privacy in Nineteenth-Century America." *Harvard Law Review* 94, no. 1 (1981): 1892–1910.

Smith, Carly Parnitzke, and Jennifer J. Freyd. "Dangerous Safe Havens: Institutional Betrayal Exacerbates Sexual Trauma." *Journal of Traumatic Stress* 26 (2013): 119–24.

Smith, Carly Parnitzke, and Jennifer J. Freyd. "Institutional Betrayal." *American Psychologist* 69, no. 6 (2014): 575–87.

Smith, Lindsay, and Kate Wells, hosts. "Gaslighting." *Believed*, NPR, November 12, 2018. https://www.npr.org/2018/11/09/666227595/gaslighting.

Smith, Rosamond. *Nemesis.* New York: Dutton, 1990.

Solnit, Rebecca. "Cassandra among the Creeps." *Harper's*, October 2014.

Spain, Sarah. "Why We Victim Blame—and Why Larry Nassar Shows We Shouldn't." *ESPN*, January 21, 2018.

Spitzberg, Brian H., Alana M. Nicastro, and Amber Cousins. "Exploring the Interactional Phenomenon of Stalking and Obsessive Relational Intrusion." *Communication Reports* 11, no. 1 (1998): 33–47.

Subbaraman, Nidhi. "Some Called It 'Vigilante Justice.' But an Anonymous Campaign Triggered a Real Investigation into a UC Santa Cruz Professor." *BuzzFeed*, May 22, 2018. https://www.buzzfeednews.com/article/nidhisubbaraman/gopal-balakrishnan-sexual-harassment-investigation.

Thomas, Ed. "Graduate Student Discovered Dead in Durham Apartment." *Duke Chronicle*, October 17, 1997.

Thompson, Crissy, and Mark A. Wood. "A Media Archeology of the Creepshot." *Feminist Studies* 18, no. 4 (2018): 560–74.

Tolentino, Jia. *Trick Mirror: Reflections on Self-Delusion.* New York: Random House, 2019.

Tomkins, Silvan. *Affect, Imagery, Consciousness* Vol. 2, *The Negative Affects.* New York: Springer, 1963.

Tuana, Nancy. "Coming to Understand: Orgasm and the Epistemology of Ignorance. *Hypathia* 19, no. 1 (2012): 194–232.

von Krafft-Ebing, Richard. *Textbook of Insanity: Based on Clinical Observations for Practitioners and Students.* Translated by Charles Gilbert Chaddock. New York: F. A. Davis, 1904.

Walkowitz, Judith. *Prostitution and Victorian Society: Women, Class, and the State.* Cambridge: Cambridge University Press, 1980.

Wang, Lin-Chi. "Final Investigative Report Re Rachael Denhollander and Larry Nassar." East Lansing: Michigan State University, Office of Institutional Equity, March 17, 2017.

Weijun Wang, Esmé. *The Collected Schizophrenias: Essays*. Minneapolis: Graywolf, 2019.

Wells, Kate. "The Day a Young Gymnast Tried to Tell MSU about Sexual Abuse." *Michigan Radio*, NPR, April 27, 2017.

White, LeeAnn. "Rebecca Latimore Felton and the Wife's Farm: The Class and Racial Politics of Gender Reform." *Georgia Historical Quarterly* 76, no. 2 (1992): 354–72.

White, Patricia. "Female Spectator, Lesbian Specter: *The Haunting*." In *Inside/Out: Lesbian Theories, Gay Theories*, edited by Diana Fuss, 142–72. New York: Routledge, 1991.

Whitman, Walt. *The Portable Walt Whitman*. Edited by Michael Warner. London: Penguin, 2003.

Will, George. "Colleges Become the Victims of Progressivism." *Washington Post*, June 6, 2014.

Will, George. "Title IX." *ABC News*, January 5, 2003. https://abcnews.go.com /ThisWeek/story?id=132569&page=1.

Will, George. "A Train Wreck Called Title IX." *Newsweek*, May 25, 2002.

Yoffe, Emily. "The College Rape Overcorrection." *Slate*, December 7, 2014.

Yoffe, Emily. "College Women: Stop Getting Drunk." *Slate*, October 15, 2013.

Yoffe, Emily. "The Problem with Campus Sexual Assault Surveys." *Slate*, September 24, 2015.

Yoffe, Emily. "The Uncomfortable Truth about Campus Sexual Assault." *Atlantic*, September 6, 2017.

INDEX

Eakins, Thomas, 37
Elliott, Emory, 29, 130–31
epistemic injustice, 90–95
epistemic violence, 103

fear, 1, 65
Federal Education Right to Privacy Act
    (FERPA), 139n7
Federici, Silvia, 71
Felton, Rebecca, 59
Ferguson, Frances, 149n33
Ferrante, Elena. See *Neapolitan* novels
fixed transference, 99
forensic examination of victims, 98
formal signifiers, 61
Fortunati, Leopoldina, 75, 143n57
Foucault, Michel, 100–102, 105
Freud, Sigmund: "A Child Is Being
    Beaten," 117; paranoia case and the-
    ory, 53–59, 67–77
Fricker, Miranda, 90

Gebser v. Lago Vista, 144n2
Gilmore, Jennifer, 87
Glissant, Edouard, 60
grievance. *See* complaint and grievance
Guattari, Félix, 99
gynecology, abusive origins of, 96

Halberstam, Jack, 56
harassment, legal definitions of, 139n2
harassment discourse: defined, 3; at
    Michigan State, 83–86; news stories,
    4; power, sexual knowledge, and, 119;
    rape culture and, 103–6; speakable
    and unspeakable forms of truth, 103;
    Title IX and, 78–80
Heddon, Deirdre, 14
Heidt, Jonathan, 85
hermeneutical injustice, 90–95
Hess, Amanda, 85
Hocquenghem, Guy, 56–57
homophobia: grief and, 115; paranoia
    and, 54–57, 72–73; work, body, and
    personal life and, 17
homosexuality: Freud on paranoia and,

53–57; patriarchy, paranoia, and, 72;
    same-sex desire in Ferrante's *Neapoli-
    tan* novels, 115–16
Howarth, Joan W., 83
Howells, Adrian, 9–18, 23–25; *An Audi-
    ence with Adrienne*, 13, 16; *May I Have
    the Pleasure*, 15–16

Ichikawa, Jonathan, 91
International Olympic Committee, 96
intimacy: "accelerated," 9; intimacy-
    seeking behavior, 26–27; queer forms
    of, 15–16; of thinking with, 11
Ion (Euripides), 101–2

Johnson, Barbara, 104
Jordan, Jan, 91

Kidder, Bill, 146n28
Kipnis, Laura, 48, 49–50, 86, 104,
    111–12, 145n10
Klages, Kathie, 93
Klein, Melanie, 20, 53, 140n2
Kristeva, Julia, 18–19

labor, productive and reproductive,
    70–76
Laing, R. D., 61–62
language: confession, 13–14; despair and
    meaning, 18–19; distancing effects of,
    13; rape as, 90, 105–6; Sedgwick on
    women and, 128–29
Lauer, Josh, 57, 60
Leaves of Grass (Whitman), 18
Lemmen, Brooke, 87–88, 94
Lester, Grant, 67–69, 142n44
Los Angeles Police Department Threat
    Management Unit (TMU), 34–36
Ludlow, Peter, 50
Lukianodd, Greg, 85
Lupton, Christina, 111

Marcus, Sharon, 90–91, 104–6
Maroney, McKayla, 93
Marx, Karl, 70, 132–33
Marxist feminism, 70–71, 75–76, 143n57